The Practitioner Inquiry Series

Marilyn Cochran-Smith and Susan L. Lytle, *SERIES EDITORS*

D1483735

Because of the Kids

FACING RACIAL AND CULTURAL DIFFERENCES IN SCHOOLS

Jennifer E. Obidah
Karen Manheim Teel

FOREWORD BY JEANNIE OAKES

TEACHERS COLLEGE PRESS

Teachers College, Columbia University
New York and London

Published by Teachers College Press, 1234 Amsterdam Avenue, New York, NY 10027

Library of Congress Cataloging-in-Publication Data

Obidah, Jennifer E.
   Because of the kids : facing racial and cultural differences in schools / Jennifer E. Obidah, Karen Manheim Teel ; foreword by Jeannie Oakes.
      p.   cm. — (The practitioner inquiry series)
   Includes bibliographical references (p.   ) and index.
   ISBN 0-8077-4013-6 (cloth : alk. paper) — ISBN 0-8077-4012-8 (pbk. : alk. paper)
      1. Multicultural education—United States.   2. Middle school teaching—United States.
   3. Teacher-student relationships—United States.   I. Teel, Karen Manheim.   II. Title.
   III. Series.
   LC1099.3 .O35   2001
   373'.01'17—dc21   00-059992

ISBN 0-8077-4012-8 (paper)
ISBN 0-8077-4013-6 (cloth)

Printed on acid-free paper

Manufactured in the United States of America
08   07   06   05   04   03   02   8   7   6   5   4   3   2

Contents

Foreword

OVER THE NEXT decade, school districts throughout the United States will need to hire more than 2 million teachers; in many places, shortages are already acute. The teacher crisis is and will continue to be particularly critical in city districts that have historically suffered a shortage of qualified teachers and routinely fill vacancies with unlicensed substitutes. The National Commission on Teaching and America's Future reported in 1998, for example, that students in schools where more than half of their peers were of color were over four times more likely to have unqualified teachers than those in schools with fewer than 10 percent students of color. Few education graduates express a desire for placements in such schools, and most that teach in them leave after just a few years. Simply put, while all students deserve well-qualified and effective teachers, students of color are least likely to have them.

However, beyond the well-publicized shortage of teachers with certification and academic preparation lies another shortage—one that may be far more devastating, and certainly one that is far less discussed. That is the woeful lack of teachers with the knowledge, skills, and disposition to teach diverse groups of low-income children effectively. Some argue that diversifying the teaching force is the only way to relieve this shortage. Teachers of color can connect with students of color in ways that white teachers cannot, and their own life experiences and perspectives can enhance their teaching effectiveness. Without doubt, we must recruit more persons of color into teaching, and then we must prepare and support them in culturally responsive ways.

Yet the fact remains that the teaching force and the young people attracted to it are predominantly white, even as the nation's schoolchildren increasingly are not. Few teacher education programs have confronted this cultural disjunction in teaching. The few that do learn quickly just how inadequate are conventional coursework and fieldwork practices. We know little and dare even less when it comes to bridging the deep divides of life experience, language, and culture between teachers and the students whose educational futures depend on their skill at reaching them.

It is this crisis in teaching and teacher preparation that African American teacher researcher Jennifer Obidah and her White colleague Karen Teel courageously confront in this book. They artfully combine their own life experiences with their empirical work as teacher researchers to examine the impact on teaching of racial differences between White teachers and African American students. The result is an impressive account of a powerful collaboration through which a White teacher, guided by her African American mentor, learns to be effective with African American students. Through their account, Obidah and Teel make real, in a way that few authors have, theories of critical multiculturalism and pedagogy that too often lie buried in a language of distance and abstraction.

In what proves to be an equally powerful story line, the authors also turn their analytic lens on the their own relationship. Doing so, they reveal both the energizing possibilities and potentially destructive tensions when teachers negotiate their own racial differences as they work. With painful honesty and moving eloquence these two dedicated and courageous teacher researchers give us a powerful story of two women reaching across America's racial divide as they work to improve teaching for the students they both care so much about. This is a book that has much to teach all who teach, and especially all of us who teach the next generation of teachers.

Jeannie Oakes

Acknowledgments

WE WOULD LIKE to thank the following people for their support and encouragement as we went on this journey together: the administrators, faculty, and staff at the middle school where we conducted this study; Karen's students over the 3 years of the study; the preservice teachers, veteran teachers, and others who have attended our presentations and given us feedback; Carol Chambers Collins, our editor, for nudging us along; Lisa Delpit, who interviewed us for the book; Edythe Boone, artist and friend; Andrea DeBruin-Parecki, for reviewing our manuscript; our husbands, Cajethan Obidah and Woody Teel; Karen's children, Liane, Katie, and Skip; and Jennifer's "rock," her mother, Norma Alleyne.

This book is dedicated to the memory of Jennifer's grandmother, Estheline (Ma May) Alleyne, and Karen's mother and father, Maggie and Jim Manheim.

Because of the Kids

Introduction

I am astounded at how often I miss exchanges between my students and me
that have racial overtones. This is such an
important issue and is so rarely addressed
by teacher educators and by schools. I ignore it, hoping it will go away or that I don't
make a big deal out of it so that it won't
get any worse.

—Karen

I thought Karen was really racist, but it's
subconscious. I feel that she wants to do
the right thing, but there are times when
her [racist behavior] occurs. And when I
tell her about it, she says that it's not true.
I feel like I'm fighting something that she
can't see. I'm fighting a ghost.

—Jennifer

HUMAN BEINGS are shaped by their life experiences. As alluded to in the preceding reflections, we teachers bring our identities to the profession: our backgrounds, cultural norms, values, beliefs, and prejudices. Even with our initial and continuing professional training, we often maintain all that we have become as a result of a myriad of life experiences.

Recently, both African American and White teacher educators have acknowledged racial and cultural differences as major stumbling blocks for White teachers in their efforts to effectively serve inner-city students (Cochran-Smith, 1995a & 1995b; Delpit, 1988, 1995; Fordham & Ogbu, 1986; King, 1991; King & Ladson-Billings, 1990; Ladson-Billings, 1995; McIntosh, 1989). Studies have examined the practices of effective African American and White teachers who teach African American students (Ladson-Billings, 1990, 1994). Other studies have analyzed the components of teacher education programs in which student teachers reflect on their perceptions of race as well as unintentional biases that influence their teaching practices (Cochran-Smith, 1995a, 1995b; Sleeter, 1993). These studies, which represent a search for answers to dilemmas faced by teachers that inevitably affect the teaching and learning that occur in their classrooms, raise sensitive issues. Still needed, however, are explorations of the possibilities for better teaching practices that result from teacher-to-teacher collaborations across race and culture.

The study on which this book is based addressed racial and cultural differences in this unique way. We, the authors, entered into a collaborative process in which Jennifer, who is African American, and Karen, who is White, investigated the impact of those differences on Karen's relationship with her primarily African American students. When we refer to racial and cultural differences, we mean differences in (a) people's perceptions of the reasons for the current condition of various groups in American society; (b) expectations for the teacher-student relationship; (c) communication styles; (d) perceptions of such concepts as respect, pride, and authority; (e) community and home environments; (f) body and spoken language; and (g) responses to Western history, art, literature, and theater, given that Western perspectives dominate school materials, assignments, and protocols in individual classrooms and schoolwide practices.

BACKGROUND OF OUR STUDY

We started working together in the fall of 1993 at a middle school where African American children from the inner city made up a majority of the student population (Obidah & Teel, 1996). Jennifer was a relatively new African American classroom teacher. She had had many previous years of working with kids outside of school. Karen, who started teaching in 1969, was a veteran White teacher with 16 years of experience teaching mostly White students.

Our study spanned a 3-year period, from 1993 until 1996. We met originally at the University of California (UC) at Berkeley in the fall of 1991, 2 years before we began our study. Jennifer had just entered the same doctoral program in education that Karen had begun in 1986. At that time, Karen was conducting the 2nd year of her dissertation research as a seventh-grade history teacher at the middle school where we eventually conducted our study.

Karen approached Jennifer at UC Berkeley and asked if she would assist an African American teacher at the middle school in developing an African American history curriculum. Karen had heard that Jennifer had received her master's in African American studies. Jennifer agreed, and one semester later, she was asked by the principal at the middle school to teach her own self-contained class of students, who had been removed from the mainstream classes because of behavior problems. Jennifer accepted the offer, and she taught two different groups of students in that class during the 1991–1992 and the 1992–1993 school years. As such, both of us were working as teachers at the same middle school before we began our study.

Each of us had our own reasons for starting this work together. When she first began her dissertation research, Karen wanted to work with African American students because of what she had learned in graduate school. She had come to believe that the "low achievement" of inner-city African American students was to a large extent the result of the teaching materials and strategies used by their teachers. Throughout the book, when we refer to the low achievement of inner-city African American students, we either add "so-called" or put the term "low achievement" in quotation marks to indicate that we question the basis for that label.

With this perspective on the education of African American children, Karen collaboratively developed alternative teaching strategies to test in her classroom for her dissertation research. These alternative strategies were based on various motivation and school-failure theories that claim in part that students do poorly in school because they have become discouraged over time by the methods and materials used by their teachers (Covington, 1984; Cummins, 1986; Heath, 1983; Marshall & Weinstein, 1984; Ogbu & Matute-Bianchi, 1986). Karen was confident that she would be as effective using these alternative strategies with her African American students as she had been with her mostly White students in past years, since she would be offering them many ways to use their strengths and talents to demonstrate their learning.

For her dissertation research, Karen documented a number of positive results with two different groups during two successive years (1990–1991 and 1991–1992). Many of her students were more motivated and performed better in her class than in their other classes, as revealed in conversations with other teachers and on students' report cards. However, despite some academic success, Karen experienced resistance from some of her students on a regular basis. Discipline was quite a problem in her classroom. Students often did not follow her rules, and many of them appeared to have very little respect for her. On several occasions, student behavioral problems curtailed Karen's abilities to implement the teaching materials and strategies that she had developed.

Karen had not experienced these kinds of problems with her White students. She felt more comfortable reprimanding them and pushing them to achieve, reinforcing the attitude and approach she believed their parents used. With her African American students, she felt somewhat alienated from the beginning. She was confused about the ways they treated her and one another, and she was reluctant to seriously reprimand them for fear of being considered a racist and of becoming even more alienated from them. Unlike her perception of her White students, her feelings in this case were that she had very little in common with her African American students and their families; she did, however, want the students to succeed in her class.

Coincidentally, during this time, she was hearing from both White and African American educators that White teachers might not ever be able to successfully work with African American students because of their racial and cultural differences. Initially, Karen rejected this notion because she felt so confident about the innovative teaching strategies she had developed and about her belief in her students' potential to succeed. However, she was dissatisfied with the high frequency of behavior problems in her classroom and with the strained relationship she had with a number of the students.

Having received her doctorate in education in May 1993, Karen wanted to return to teaching the next year at the same middle school. Her goal was to become as effective a teacher of African American students as she had been of White students in the past, but she was not sure how to overcome the difficulties she had experienced with her African American students. She surmised that a possible way to improve her teaching was to seek guidance from an African American teacher whom she respected.

Karen was confident enough in herself as a teacher to allow an outside observer into her classroom on a regular basis. On the recommendation of a White colleague in graduate school, she had observed Jennifer at the middle school during both the 1991–1992 and the 1992–1993 school years and found her to be a very effective teacher with the students.

Our position is that "effective teaching" is demonstrated when most of the students (1) are motivated to succeed; (2) have a positive relationship with the teacher; (3) are engaged in the lesson most of the time with very little resistance; (4) feel challenged, supported, and interested in the curriculum; and (5) are showing improvement in all skill areas and in subject matter knowledge. In addition, we assert that effective teachers believe that their students are capable of high achievement and are constantly encouraging them to do well. In Karen's view, Jennifer met the criteria of an effective teacher, so she approached her with the idea of a collaboration.

Over the years of teaching at the middle school, Jennifer had observed that every day a disproportionate number of African American students were sent from classrooms into the hallways, or referred to the counselors or assistant principal for misbehavior. Jennifer wondered how these students were being educated if they were absent from class so frequently. She also wondered about the nature of the misbehaviors that students committed and if these students had similar problems in other teachers' classes.

During the second semester at the school, Jennifer had the opportunity to act as school counselor for one week, and she used this time to explore some of her questions regarding students' misbehaviors and subsequent referrals. She learned that (1) the majority of students referred to the counselors and assistant principal were African American males; (2) many of the behavior problems were described by the students, in their conversations with her, as racially motivated on the part of the teachers; and (3) certain White teachers in particular were referring the students.

Jennifer had overheard these White teachers in the teachers' lunchroom talking disparagingly or with exasperation about African American students at the middle school. These were the same teachers whose attitudes and actions toward their students had been perceived as racist and mentioned to Jennifer by African American teachers' aides, resource teachers, and security personnel who had observed these teachers. A series of enlightening incidents with some of these teachers occurred as the year progressed.

At a faculty meeting, Jennifer brought up the matter of large numbers of African American students being sent out to the hallways from classrooms. One White male teacher loudly responded that many of the African American students were uncivilized, and if they chose to act like animals, he was not putting up with their behavior and would send them out. He ended by saying that once these students were trained they could return to his classroom. His remarks prompted a heated argument with Jennifer, who was incensed with his referral to African American students as "uncivilized animals."

Two key exchanges occurred that summer between Jennifer and two of the other White teachers who frequently referred African American students from their classrooms. During a professional development course in which Jennifer and these teachers participated, Jennifer learned in conversations with one of the teachers that as a teenager he had been bullied incessantly by African American boys. He admitted that he still carried that wariness of these students with him, hence his intolerance for their minor infractions. While sharing one of the course assignments, Jennifer was stirred by the writing of the other teacher, in which the teacher described the wonderful relationship she shared with her children, which led to her love of teaching and nurturing children's growth. When questioned by Jennifer about her relationship with her African American students, this teacher admitted that she felt incapable of developing the kind of relationship with this group of students that she had written about because they were so "different" from her.

These experiences made Jennifer wonder if teachers who held such views about African American students could ever be capable of effectively teaching these students. She believed that teachers' perceptions of the racial and cultural differences between them and their students were major contributors to the problems they were having. Thus, when Karen approached Jennifer with the idea of a collaboration, Jennifer saw this as an opportunity to view firsthand, and over a period of time, how one White teacher's perceptions of African American students influenced her ability to effectively teach and interact with them. She was also interested in seeing whether, over time, negative views could be changed for the better.

Karen asked Jennifer if she would be willing to come into her classroom the following year (1993–1994) on a weekly basis to observe her with her students and to give her advice on how to modify the teaching strategies she was using to more successfully serve the students. Jennifer agreed to participate in such a study as long as we also looked at the role that racial and cultural differences between Karen and her students played in her interactions with them. Thus our study began with these two goals: to improve Karen's teaching practices and to examine the impact of racial and cultural differences on the teaching and learning that occurred in her classroom. Karen agreed to look at the impact of these racial and cultural differences in her classroom, though, at that time, she was certain that those differences were not causing her problems with the students.

BECAUSE OF THE KIDS

Jennifer anticipated that racial and cultural differences between Karen and her African American students would indeed have an impact on the teacher-student relationship and on the students' academic achievement. After several pivotal experiences during our study, Karen, too, began to recognize those differences as contributing to the problems with her students. However, we had no idea that racial and cultural differences *between us* would become a potential threat to our research project, and they did. In addition, we did not anticipate the extent to which our work to understand and resolve the differences between us would alter and deepen our relationship with each other and change our lives.

As such, as the research progressed, the focus expanded. Not only were we examining the racial and cultural differences between Karen and her students, and subsequently developing more effective classroom practices with the students; we also began to reflect on our process of learning to communicate with each other across racial and cultural boundaries. In this book we detail the challenges that we faced as women from different races and cultures, occupying the roles of teacher and researcher, attempting to generate concrete ways that Karen could more effectively educate her African American students.

We discuss in this volume our different backgrounds and philosophies, the development and importance of our relationship to the study as it evolved over the 3 years, and the influence the study had on our thinking and teaching practices. We came to realize that the reason we persevered in overcoming the barriers between us was *because of the kids*— hence the title of our book. It was our belief in the potential of these students and our commitment to promoting their success in school that gave us the strength and determination to complete our work together. It is our hope that the findings from this study will not only add to the existing body of literature, but will also encourage other teachers to collaboratively explore these issues, toward the higher academic achievement of African American students in our schools.

OUTLINE OF BOOK

In chapter 1 we tell our "herstories": stories of our childhoods growing up in very different parts of the United States. In chapter 2 we describe our history of working with African American students. We talk in chapter 3 about the challenges of going the distance, persevering with this work even though our perspectives clashed time after time. In chapter 4, we discuss our different perceptions across race and class that contributed to our disagreements over student behavior, teacher authority, and discipline. In chapters 3 and 4, we discuss the ways in which Karen changed in her approach to her students, resulting in a more positive relationship with them and in higher student achievement. We give specific examples from the processes in which we engaged as we sorted through our differences. Our analysis in chapter 4 is based on responses by each of us to the other's observation notes and numerous lengthy dialogues that were taped and transcribed over the course of the first year.

In chapter 5 we frame our experiences in terms of what we now reflect on as risks we took as two teachers investigating the consequences of racial and cultural differences in Karen's classroom. Each of us writes about what we perceived as our own risks along the way, including the ways that we each thought we could be negatively affected by this work—both personally and professionally.

Chapter 6 is based on an interview that Lisa Delpit conducted with us. This interview focuses on the issues she raised in her own work addressing racial and cultural differences between teachers and students (1988, 1992a, 1992b, 1995) and highlights nuances of the cultural conflict between us and our development as more effective teachers of African American students.

We gave chapter 7 the title "For Those Who Dare" to reflect the often challenging nature of our experiences. This process took a strong commitment to the students, trust in each other, and patience with the process to overcome the obstacles we faced. In this chapter we make some recommendations about how other classroom teachers, teacher educators, and professors might develop collaborations like ours—across different races and cultures—in their own particular contexts, to improve the education of African American students.

CHAPTER 1

"Herstories" Shaping Research and Teaching Practices

> Being Black isn't all that matters to my being a good teacher.
>
> —Jennifer

> I didn't think that my being a White woman mattered.
>
> —Karen

IN THIS CHAPTER, we begin our personal "herstories" that describe our complex identities—Jennifer, an African American woman of Caribbean descent from a working-class background, and Karen, a White American woman from a middle-class background now living in an upper middle-class environment. We discuss how our identities were shaped by our environment, cultures, and races and by the societal structures in which we lived. Our herstories begin with narratives of our childhood memories—including our neighborhoods and schools—and conclude with our college and graduate school experiences.

CHILDHOOD MEMORIES

JENNIFER

I was not born in the United States. I was born in Barbados, a small island in the West Indies. As an adolescent I relocated with my parents to New

York City. My father had come some years before to set up a home in
the United States for his family, and my mother joined him in March
1980. A few months after my mother arrived in New York City, my
parents sent for my brother and me, the youngest of their children.

I remember my brother and myself sitting on the plane trying to
imagine our new lives. We had told all of our friends that we were going
away for good (i.e., we were going to live there, and we probably would
not return to the island for years). We joked about what would happen
if we didn't like it and then decided to return to the island, after announc-
ing that we were going for good. But how could we not like it? It was
the United States of America, where the streets were paved with gold.
In fact, we had given away practically all of our clothes to our friends
because we knew we would be buying new ones almost immediately in
the United States. These positive thoughts filled our minds throughout
the 4-hour flight to New York but were cast into question not long after
we deplaned.

Our mom and dad picked us up in their not-so-new car, and as we
drove from the airport through Queens into Brooklyn, the sight of run-
down, burned-out, abandoned brick apartment buildings rising from lit-
tered sidewalks was my first indication that everyone in the United States
was not economically prosperous. That perception contrasted with what
I had learned from watching the imported American shows on Barbados
television. And things kept going downhill the farther away we traveled
from the airport to our new home.

My parents lived in a basement apartment of the building where my
father was the superintendent. The door we came through from the street
was in fact the door to the basement of the building, where electrical
wires swung openly from a low ceiling, and the boiler stood surrounded
by surplus furniture and appliances from apartments refurbished for new
tenants. That was my brother's and my first sight of home. We walked
past this open space to another door, the door to our apartment. I was
relieved to see a home, as only my mom could make, waiting for me
behind the second door. That night, as we lay in beds across from each
other, my brother and I quietly laughed about our first impressions of
where we now lived and whispered our regret about giving away all of
our clothes.

My first 2 weeks in the United States were spent in TV land. On the
island, television began at 4 p.m. and ended at 11 p.m. I was amazed that
in the United States television came on 24 hours a day! I was fascinated
by American life as presented through television and enthralled with
shows that featured more Black than White characters. During those first
2 weeks of life in the United States, I watched TV from 11 a.m. until 5

the following morning, when I became too sleepy to watch any more. As soon as I woke up, though, which was around 11 a.m. the next day, I would start to watch again. Meanwhile my brother had already ventured out into the world. He had already started to hang out on the streets of Brooklyn with other "Bajan-Yankees" (as Barbadian immigrants referred to each other).

My brother attended Wingate High School to finish his education. Since I already had finished high school in Barbados, I went to work to help my parents. It was becoming clear to my brother and me that my parents were financially unstable. College was not even a thought then, since things looked so bleak.

I went to work as a full-time babysitter for a young White family who lived in Queens, earning $150 a week. This was a lot of money for a young West Indian girl, especially when I converted the U.S. currency to Barbadian (the conversion rate was and still is two Barbadian dollars to one U.S. dollar). It was only after working that I started buying clothes to replace the ones I had given away. Once I had my own money to spend, I started to appreciate living in New York City.

But I was also dealing with the fact of an unhappy family. In addition to their financial problems, my parents' marriage was failing. I was actually more relieved than sad when my parents separated, because the arguing stopped. My mother, my brother, and I moved from Brooklyn Heights to Bedford-Stuyvesant.

After life in Barbados, the streets of Bedford-Stuyvesant in New York offered a new kind of education. I learned how to talk and walk the streets of "Bed-Stuy, Do or Die!" Life had a dangerous edge. The potential for emotional explosions was always there. These explosions occur to serve as salve for the crush of oppressions—both external and self-imposed—that permeate the existence of human beings in poor inner-city neighborhoods. This rage, once exposed, could result, at best, in a fight or, at worst, in someone getting killed.

I remember my teenage friends Vinny, Sabu, and Elvis. I saw Vinny one day after not seeing him for a long time, only to learn of his death in a shoot-out 2 weeks later. I remember Sabu, who was stabbed to death in a fight. I remember Elvis, who got shot for two dollars at a gambling table by his friend—our friend—Darius. Living in the Bedford-Stuyvesant neighborhood of New York City was where my knowledge of living intimately with frequent homicide began. In our neighborhood we were respected for our knowledge and awareness of this and other elements of street life, and we continued to live in spite of the dangers. And we had fun.

I remember summers in New York with my "homegirls" (childhood girlfriends), staying up all night long on the weekends in the grip of summer heat that made any attempts at a good night's sleep impossible. We would hang out on the steps of the brownstone where I lived, telling jokes that induced tearstained, stomachaching laughter. We talked and laughed long into the night. We were often startled by the lightening in the sky and then resigned to the heat and humidity promised by the sun's rising. I remember the block parties: little girls practicing their dance routines weeks and weeks before, to then "turn it out" at the party. Grandmothers and grandfathers, mothers and fathers, sons and daughters congregated. A block party was a culminating abundance of food, laughter, and fun. I enjoyed the good and coped with the bad of my life in Bed-Stuy. I didn't think of my neighborhood as a place to get out of. It was home.

KAREN

I am a White woman, 54 years old, and have been teaching since I was 23. I grew up in an all-White, middle-class neighborhood in the 1950s in the central California city of Fresno. My family and neighborhood could be compared to the idyllic families portrayed in the popular TV shows *Ozzie and Harriet, Leave it to Beaver,* and *Father Knows Best.* My father was a salesman, my mother a housewife, and we were a family of five. I had one older and one younger brother. My mother was a volunteer in the schools as we all went through them. She was also the leader of my Brownie and Girl Scout troops for several years and volunteered her time in the elementary school library.

Over the years of my youth, my mother passed on significant beliefs and values. Albeit from a safe distance, she was an advocate for the downtrodden. Whenever she saw any person or animal being mistreated, she became incensed. One of the most important individuals in her framework was herself. She demanded respect from everyone around her and urged me to love and respect myself first and never allow others to compromise my integrity or principles. I remember her saying that no one would ever walk on her or mistreat her in any way. She was passionate about this critical need for self-respect, and she instilled this belief in me. One of the quotes she often cited was from *Hamlet:* "To thine own self be true and as night follows day thou canst be false to any man" (her version).

Typically, on summer days during my elementary school years, I would play with two school friends in my neighborhood, both of whom had swimming pools. We would while away the days playing cards, basking in the sun, and swimming in one of the pools. On summer evenings, I was often out in the street with the neighbors playing Capture the Flag and Hide and Go Seek. As I grew up in Fresno, I made friends who lived in other neighborhoods across town. During the summer, I began riding my bike to their homes or to the school, where we would spend time together. In my neighborhood, there were no drugs, no gun shots, and no crime that I was aware of. We never locked our doors—even at night. I remember a childhood without stress, with family stability, and with fun, carefree times.

In that same neighborhood I went to local elementary, junior high, and high schools in the late 1950s and early 1960s. I was a pom-pom girl, a cheerleader, and was elected to several class offices. The student population at all of the schools I attended was almost all White. The only reason I knew there was an African American community somewhere in Fresno was because our athletic teams competed against their junior high and high school teams. I had little or no other exposure to African American people as I was growing up in Fresno. You could almost say that they were invisible to me or in a world apart from mine. I never needed to visit their community, and I never did. I believed at that time that such separation was just the way it was. I did not question our separate worlds. I knew nothing about the African American community, and I learned nothing (that I can remember) about African Americans in school.

I do not remember my parents discussing the civil rights movement when I was in high school, from 1960 to 1964, or when I was in college, from 1964 to 1969. I remember very little about Dr. Martin Luther King, Jr. I think my family watched the protests in the South on television with interest, but none of us considered participating in any way. I believe that my mom supported the cause of the southern Blacks as she always did when people around the world were victims of prejudice, hatred, and injustice. She was not an activist, however. She was very patriotic and believed that the government was basically quite sound and would do something about the inequities in our society through legal channels. Her top priority was for my brothers and me to have an idyllic childhood.

I loved school. Every day I looked forward to going to school, and I relished the whole experience: the routine, the homework, and just about everything else. I never found the teachers or the work to be boring. I always thought that I should do my work, try to get A's, and do my best according to what teachers expected and asked me to do. I was never disrespectful to the teachers, because I admired them. I had friends who were excellent students, but they were not my best friends. I liked the kids who were a bit rebellious because they were more fun and interesting, but I always toed the line myself. I wanted to be one of the top students in my school so I would make my parents proud and so I could go to a prestigious college or university.

COLLEGE EXPERIENCES

JENNIFER

After one year I left my job working for the family in Queens and started to work part-time providing after-school care for an older White child in Manhattan. Life had settled down at home. My mother was working steadily by this time, so I applied to, and was accepted at, Hunter College of the City University of New York.

Unlike most of my friends, I started college in "the city," as those of us from the borough of Brooklyn referred to the borough of Manhattan. I moved out of the neighborhood, but I returned often to see my mother, some older people in the neighborhood whose houses I used to visit, and some of my friends. By my sophomore year, all five of my homegirls were pregnant. Three of them were sisters. Tam, the youngest sibling and the youngest girl in our group, was 14 when she had her first baby and 16 when she had her second. And Tam could not read. Yo and Stefan were addicted to crack, and Drew and Goofy were in jail. Others, like me, left the old neighborhood.

Underlying my decision to pursue higher education was a desire to enhance what knowledge I already had about the schooling of African American youth. Immigrating from Barbados, I felt somewhat limited in my knowledge of African American history. These African Americans were very different from me in their expressions of Blackness. I felt the need for a wider, historical perspective of these people who were Black like me, yet very different from me and from the West Indian community transplanted in New York City. Upon graduating from Hunter College with a bachelor of arts in sociology and with high honors, I entered Yale University to complete a master's degree in African American studies.

I left New York City without a legacy of graduate school wisdom that might have been imparted to me if I had had family members who were graduates of higher education. No one in my family and no one else I had known had ever attended graduate school, and I was the first in my family. My elders only knew that it was "different." I was sent to Yale with all that they had to give me: their pride in my acceptance to Yale University, their prayers for me not to fail, and their expectations and hopes that I would graduate.

The sobering reality of difference was the first fact of graduate school at Yale. New Haven was unlike New York City, and the majority-White population at the university greatly contrasted—both in race and socioeconomic status—with the majority-Black population of the Brooklyn neighborhoods. Unhappily, during my first year, any efforts I undertook to form alliances with members of the Black communities of New Haven that surrounded the university—from attending the neighborhood clubs and volunteering at the local high school to getting acquainted with a family through courtship with a local guy—were tempered by my transient status and affiliation with Yale. Meanwhile, my actual alienation from fellow students paralleled the alienating nature of the town-and-gown relationship between the Yale and Greater New Haven communities.

Even the other Black students and I were dissimilar. We were all Black but they were rich. My "What's up!?" greeting was as discomforting to them as their formally returned greeting of "Hi Jennifer, how are you?" was to me. The difference in styles of greeting each other was a small indication of the larger class differences between myself and other Black students who attended Yale. My Brooklyn talk was even more problematic in the university's classrooms.

It seemed that compared with other students, I spoke with too much passion, too many exclamations, and too many anecdotal descriptions. Patronizing sympathy from both fellow graduate students and professors usually started with, "So the point you're making is . . . " followed by an explanation that was never quite what I had intended in my original version. I realized that to these students and professors, it was as if I spoke a foreign language with no available instruments for translation into their own language. I resorted to reading, writing, and listening as my primary forms of classroom participation.

By November of my first year, the university's buildings felt like cold inaccessible fortresses surrounded by dungeonlike dormitories. I lived only for the infrequent revitalizing visits to the old neighborhood, where self-doubt—the primary emotion I felt within the elm-encircled walls of the university—would be replaced with the overconfidence of one who was treated as special at home.

Unfortunately, I had also become a transient guest in the old neighborhood. The lives of my friends of old had taken different paths and I no longer felt the need to locate them, but I felt the loss of that need. The neighborhood had changed, and I had changed even more. The new lens of awareness acquired through my education at Yale, a lens through which I began to gaze upon the old neighborhood, dampened my sense of belonging and even my desire to belong. Simultaneously, however, I distrusted the people and the scholarship that engendered this critique of familiar people, places, and living conditions. I distrusted this Ivy League education that made me feel uncomfortable in a place filled with memories I still found comforting. My memories were stained by my education. As time passed, the old people of the neighborhood became my only motivation for visiting Bed-Stuy.

My 2nd year at Yale was much better than the first. During this year there were sporadic moments when thoughts, ideas, expressions, and events combined to form valuable learning experiences. I learned about the slavery of Africans in the United States; I learned about the historic, unfulfilled promises America made to its citizens of African descent; and I learned about the many African American scholars of sociology, psychology, law, and literature who have documented the African American experience in the United States.

Other important learning experiences came from my involvement with the African American Cultural Center at the university. I became involved at the center as the director of the Black Graduate Network (BGN), although I confess that, initially, my motives derived from my need to alleviate the pain and isolation I had felt since my first year. I regained my self-confidence through coordinating events for graduate students. Events such as lectures, discussions, African dance classes, and fund-raising parties helped to create alliances between the Black graduate students at Yale, and they afforded me some sense of community, since my former notion had become a casualty of higher education. My success and graduation with a master's degree from Yale were driven by my determination not to disappoint my elders. After 2 years at Yale, I decided to pursue a doctorate at Berkeley.

KAREN

From my high school in Fresno, I went to UC Berkeley in 1964 and joined an all-White sorority that did not then allow minority students. During the first semester of my freshman year, I attended classes in the midst of the "free speech" movement (Goines, 1993). Protesters were gathered together on the steps of Sproul Plaza to hear and rally behind speeches about the oppressive nature of the administration at the university. More and more restrictive laws were passed by the board of regents of the university, regulating both speech making and the distribution of controversial literature. This movement was taking place at the same time as the civil rights movement in the South, and several of the protesters had been involved earlier in that movement as well. As one Berkeley student explained his perspective: "A student who has been chased by the KKK in Mississippi is not easily intimidated by academic bureaucrats" (Goines, 1993, p. 15).

While these events that would shake the foundations of American society were occurring, I was aware of them and talked about them with my sorority sisters and with my dates, but in general, I was uninvolved and uninterested in the causes. I believed that the issues at stake were irrelevant to me, and I considered the protesters to be mostly individuals from outside the university who were bored with their lives and needed some excitement—something to motivate them and to get involved in. I didn't understand why anyone would care about who came to speak on campus. I couldn't have cared less about the political scene on campus nor around the world.

After going to school in Florence and in Paris, and then traveling to other cities in Europe during my junior year, however, I returned to UC Berkeley with a broader perspective on the world and a new interest in politics. Ironically, despite my apathetic attitude toward politics during my freshman and sophomore years, I had become very interested in comparative government and international relations while living over-seas. In my senior year, I concentrated on the governments in communist countries. I was particularly fascinated by the relationship between a country's leaders and its citizens and the notion of individual freedom.

I also read the book *Black Like Me* (Griffin, 1960), my first look at the discrepancies in American society between the lives of White and African American people. I was shocked and appalled at what I learned from the White author's experiences when he disguised himself as an African American man and traveled in the South while the Jim Crow laws were still in effect. I knew that African American people lived in their own communities, but I thought that such separation was their choice, and I never imagined what they experienced when they entered White commu-nities—especially in the South.

At this point all I did to express my concern about such inequities in American society was to align myself with the Democratic Party and to involve myself on a limited basis with the presidential election of 1968. I was horrified with the assassinations of Dr. Martin Luther King, Jr., and Robert Kennedy, events that heightened my awareness of the intensity of the political differences between various groups in American society. From my childhood experiences and my college studies, I had come to believe in equal opportunity for all American citizens and to support government leaders who not only expressed the same views but also took action, such as initiating or supporting civil rights legislation. I was aware of discrimination in our society, and strongly opposed it and supported any efforts by the government to eradicate it.

Because of my interest in international relations and my opposition to communism, I wanted to work for the Central Intelligence Agency or in the diplomatic services, and so I majored in political science. During one of my political science classes in my senior year, a representative from the State Department gave a presentation about the opportunities available in the government. This was 1968. After class I approached him and told him about my interests. He told me not to bother, because women didn't get those kinds of positions in the government. Since I was rather accepting of the status quo at that point in my life, I did not question the system, and did not continue the discussion with him. Based on that conversation, I decided not to pursue a career in the government, because, as a woman, I was convinced that I would not be hired.

Around this time, I became engaged to a young man who wanted to attend law school. I decided to go into teaching. It wasn't what I thought I wanted to do professionally in the long run, but since it was a career open to women, I thought it would be a good way to support my husband while he was working on his career. I believed that once he was established, I could pursue the career of my choice. He also was interested in participating in politics, which I saw as a way I could get into the political scene as a woman—as the politician's wife.

I entered a one-year, secondary teacher credential program at UC Berkeley for the following year (1968–1969). Since my undergraduate major was political science and my minor French, I completed my student teaching in San Francisco's East Bay area in one middle school history class, in one high school government class, and in one middle school French class. My experiences in this program were very positive in that I found teaching to be challenging, exciting, and creative. I also enjoyed the independence afforded teachers in the classroom in the choices we have of teaching methods and materials. My favorite aspect of the teaching experience, however, was watching my students grow and make progress in their skills and knowledge with my guidance.

I realized during this year of teacher training that I wanted classroom teaching to be my career. Consequently, even though my husband decided not to go to law school at this point and went to work as a banker, I continued to explore teaching possibilities over the summer of 1969 after I had received my teaching credential. Toward the end of the summer, I was offered and accepted a full-time position, teaching seventh grade world history in a school district in the San Francisco East Bay area.

SUMMARY

Thus far, we've tried to convey the individual experiences that have had a significant impact on our work as teachers of African American students. From Karen's life emerge themes of unfamiliarity with African American children and their culture as she embarked on her teaching career in 1969. From Jennifer's life are themes of familiarity and empathy with African American children through her own lived experiences.

Simply put, Karen's life excluded the need for interactions with African Americans. Karen's total lack of familiarity with African American children, with their families, and with their culture, was confirmed as normal and acceptable not only by her neighbors but also by the images portrayed on television and by the school knowledge she acquired. None of these contexts indicated to Karen a necessity to know or interact with people other than those who looked like her. As Karen noted earlier, it was as if the African American community in her town was "invisible" to her. Karen's life exemplifies how separation between the races is such a normalized aspect of American society that White Americans are oblivious to it. We argue that this oblivion occurs because the lives of many White Americans are unaffected by the absence of African Americans, so that interactions of many Whites with African Americans are neither desired nor sought. Perhaps this separateness would also not be a problem for African Americans if it weren't for the omnipresence of White people in the lives of African Americans through social, political, and economic structures, some of which are oppressive to African Americans in their day-to-day lived experiences. Thus it becomes important for African Americans to always be conscious of and to make White Americans aware of the roles that they play in maintaining such a society. As we continue our "herstories" in chapter 2, we describe our early years of working with African American students.

Perceptions of African American Students

There was more to my friends and my students than the perception of them as problem students within schools. Their problems did not encompass all of who they were as human beings. Yet in their interactions with society, and schools in particular, they were often viewed only through the lens of their problems. Teachers equipped with this one-dimensional lens are incapable of effectively teaching these students.

—Jennifer

All my perceptions of African American students at this point in time were based on assumptions I had about them that came from what I had seen or heard from the media about life in the inner city and from the students' placement in lower tracked classes. I assumed that these students were so-called underachievers because of their own shortcomings, which were the result of their upbringing.

—Karen

CONTINUING OUR STORIES, we trace some of the evolving themes that influenced our perceptions of African American students. With Karen we also describe how her perspectives on these students shifted during her years in graduate school. We conclude with the story of meeting each other and the start of our collaboration.

WORKING WITH AFRICAN AMERICAN CHILDREN

JENNIFER

Working with African American children was not as much a conscious decision for me as it was a way of life. I've worked with Black children all my life. Black children were my friends. They are members of my family. The majority of my teachers were Black. Some of them lived in the same neighborhood as I did, and they knew my mother and father. Neither my parents nor my teachers would settle for less than my best academically. In fact, I was in a lot of trouble in my house if I placed less than in the top-ten list of students in the class. To be "low achieving" academically was never an option, nor an expectation, for me.

I grew up in very different circumstances in the early years of my life from those of my friends in New York City. For instance, while I was a child in the Caribbean, the possible homicide of my family and friends was not an occurrence I could have envisioned. I took for granted that my friends and I would finish school, grow up, have children, and live lives similar to those of our parents.

However, my coming to the United States and living in the Bedford-Stuyvesant section of Brooklyn, as mentioned earlier, made me aware not only of terrible realities such as frequent incidents of homicide in African American neighborhoods, but also of the limiting and at times negative expectations of African American people that were held by mainstream American society. I found myself constantly fighting against other people's limitations on me. For instance, upon my entering a store, the clerks often treated me as a potential shoplifter rather than a welcomed customer. Attending school, I was more often addressed by teachers as a possible failure than as a potentially successful student. Negotiating against such limiting expectations could have hampered my academic success without the strong foundation with which I came to the United States. I didn't think I experienced any discrimination and prejudices because I was a woman, although on occasion, that may have been the case. I firmly believed that it was because I was Black. It became wearisome over time, my having to constantly and defensively strategize my existence in latently hostile environments. However, in my case this way of being began when I was an older adolescent. For African American students, it often begins at birth.

I've worked with Black students in some sort of teaching and learning capacity since the age of 15. My work began with children in the Caribbean, when I started working with adolescents as a camp counselor while I myself was a teenager. Despite my age, I was acknowledged as the leader/teacher in my interactions with other students. I respected, asked for, and relied on students' critique of how good a teacher I was, because at that time I was sometimes only 2 years older than those in my charge, so that what we knew—our sources of knowledge—were not exceedingly different. I just happened to be the designated leader. These lessons of mutual respect and shared knowledge are integral to my work with children today.

In my junior year of college I started working at community centers in after-school programs serving African American youth from Harlem. I worked with these young people in the role of counselor, tutor, or teacher. I was always drawn to those kids, who reminded me of my old crew of friends in Bed-Stuy. Through these experiences, another education began for me. I finally saw what might have been the experience of my friends in junior high school. I would observe the kids with their friends on the playing areas of the center: their confidence, laughter, quick retorts, dry humor, and spontaneous talk back and forth with each other. Then the time came for the kids to be "taught" by me.

When they entered the classroom, all of the liveliness I observed earlier would be replaced by quietness or sullen unresponsiveness. These students became wary of being called on to "know," to be responsible for the school knowledge lodged in the curricular texts we covered. This was knowledge that these kids perceived as estranged from the realities of their daily life. I became determined to make the teaching and learning environment a different experience for these children.

To these students, I was Black like them, but I was also a "teacher." As their teacher, I wielded an authority that potentially threatened to impose on them a negative student identity that was in opposition to their own strong sense of themselves. My students' sullen resistance indicated to me that authority was inefficient as a premise for effective teacher-student relationships. I worked hard to change the classroom environment. In time, not only was I no longer threatening to my students, but I also managed to create a safe and motivating learning environment. My resolve to improve the academic achievement of these children, and my concern about their overall disengagement with schooling, influenced my decision to apply to graduate school.

As we mentioned in the introduction, during my first year in the doctoral program at UC Berkeley, I met Karen. Somehow she had learned that I had a master's degree in African American studies. One of the other world history teachers at Karen's school was teaching an African American history class for the first time that year and expressed to Karen the need for some collaboration. Karen talked to me, and I was happy to help the teacher. I eventually ended up working with this teacher in his class on a weekly basis. Through this work the administrators of the school got to know me, and I was asked by the principal to teach the "Cluster Academy"—a class of 25 students who were perceived by the rest of the school community to have major academic and behavioral problems.

I started teaching part-time at the middle school. In my class I met African American youths from poor neighborhoods with very similar problems and responses to school learning as had my students in East Harlem. Talking with mothers as well as kids, I heard stories of children being suspended in first grade. First grade! I heard and saw mothers trying to have their children kept back in school because they knew that their children could not read or write. This was a difficult choice for parents, especially in light of the fear that their children might fall further behind academically. However, in some instances, the choice was not the parents' to make. The school would refuse to retain some students because of behavioral problems. They wanted these students to be someone else's problem.

I would visit all of the "alternative classrooms" in the middle school and see that the students were often African American youths from the most economically disadvantaged neighborhoods in the inner city. As a teacher, I was prepared to handle almost any problem with my students right there in my classroom, because I so distrusted the system's way of handling them. These kids, known in the school as Cluster kids, were already labeled as having behavior problems. I did not want to further confirm that label outside my classroom. Although some of my students' behaviors were difficult, I felt that they still were manageable by me, the teacher.

However, as a new teacher, I experienced many troubling moments in my classroom. A version of the explosive anger that existed in my old neighborhood was also a product of the environment from which my new students came. I remember the first time that a fight occurred in my classroom. This was a fight between two boys I knew to be friends. As the fight erupted and was spurred on by the surrounding group of students, I impulsively jumped in between the two boys (an action I was always advised as a new teacher *not* to do). I was yelling as I tried to push them apart: "You will *not* disrespect my classroom this way! This is my

classroom! My house! If you want to act like this go to your own house!"
The boys' surprise at my taking their fighting so personally ended the
fight faster than any physical efforts that I could have used.

I lectured the entire class on how bad I thought fighting was, and I
voiced my concern about the possible outcomes of uncontrollable anger.
I heatedly stressed to the onlooking 14-year-olds:

> "In 3 years it'll be a gun you're using to fight with!" To my im-
> mense surprise the class burst into laughter and one student re-
> plied: "Ms. Johnson, it's already a gun!"

I laughed along with the students and for the rest of the class we
discussed the violence they coped with daily. As time passed I had fewer
disruptions in my classroom. The teacher-student relationship of mutual
respect that developed between me and my students also helped to create
a space for effective teaching and learning to flourish in my classroom. I
relished my students' small and frequent steps of academic success, which
I detail elsewhere (Alleyne Johnson [Obidah], 1995b).

Still, I was sobered by the fact that violence had become so prevalent
in my students' lives. Moreover, knowledge about guns and fear of dying
from a gunshot wound were the realities of these students, who were
much younger than my childhood friends and I had been when gun
violence began to affect our lives. The experiences of my students and
the memories of my friends motivated me to develop teaching practices
that brought the two worlds of home and school together with more
positive results for the children.

There was more to my friends in my old neighborhood and my
students than the problems that they had. Their problems did not encompass all of who they were as human beings—for example, their joys, their
hopes, and their dreams. Yet in their interactions with society, and schools
in particular, they were often viewed only through the lens of their problems. Teachers equipped with this one-dimensional lens are incapable of
effectively teaching these students.

During this time, I keenly identified with my students' predicament,
because I also perceived that similar views were being held about me by
some of my professors at Berkeley. As a result, I was becoming more and
more removed from my own schooling experience. Karen will tell you
that graduate school helped her to realize the potential of her African
American students. In contrast, going to Berkeley made me doubt my
knowledge about the education of children, African American children
in particular, that I had acquired through lived experiences. In those first
2 years of my doctoral studies, unnecessary polarities emerged. I was

going to school to learn the discipline of education and at the same time I was teaching in an urban public middle school. I went back and forth from the classroom where I was a teacher of so-called at-risk students to a graduate classroom where I was the at-risk student.

Making connections between teaching in an urban classroom and learning educational theories was unimaginably difficult. The knowledge I was gaining from my experience as a public school teacher was difficult to bring into the discussions in the university classrooms. I felt unsure about this knowledge because it was constantly invalidated in the university setting. Beginning my work with Karen in a relationship where my unique perspective was validated helped me to remember, value, and appreciate my homegrown intellect along with the knowledge I acquired in the university. Karen's appreciation for my help and our subsequent success in her classroom became one of my rewards for continuing this work.

KAREN

When I started teaching, all of the students at the junior high school were White, mainly from middle-class families. In the 1970s, the school board decided on a busing policy under which students could transfer from one school to another on a volunteer-only basis. Consequently, a few years later, some African American students started coming from the inner city to the school where I was teaching.

At that time there was tracking in the district, based on test scores, grades in upper elementary school, and teacher recommendations. The three tracks in my school were "gifted," "average," and "low achieving." I was offered a few gifted classes, and, since it was considered a privilege to have these students, teachers were expected to teach some of the "less desirable" groups as well. Much to my surprise, however, I found that I really liked teaching the lowest tracked students. I enjoyed their boundless energy, spontaneity, curiosity, willingness to take risks, sense of humor, and honesty.

At that time—as hard as it may be to believe—I didn't think that anything was wrong with the fact that most of the students in the lowest tracks were African Americans who had come to my school from the inner city. At the time I believed that these students probably were slower, that they just wouldn't understand the material as easily as the higher tracked students. I assumed that because they were put in the lower tracks they weren't as "smart." Consequently, I felt that I needed to teach them differently from how I taught the "gifted" students.

I designed simpler lessons for them, believing that such materials were what they needed and were all that they could handle. I did not push them in their thinking, because I believed that the best form of instruction for them would be activities such as filling out worksheets about a short passage in a book I gave them or about a film I showed them. I also gave them simple maps to complete, based on information given in their book. I avoided complicated assignments that would require independent work inside and outside of class, and I avoided discussions during class that demanded higher levels of thinking and that might get out of hand. I thought the students would feel inept with these more sophisticated kinds of activities and that both the projects and the discussions would be a waste of their time and energy.

All my perceptions of African American students at this time were based on my assumptions about them, which came from what I had seen or heard in the media about life in the inner city and from the students' placement in these lower tracks. I assumed that these students were so-called underachievers because of their own shortcomings, which were the result of their upbringing. I am referring to shortcomings such as poor reading and writing skills and a lack of the motivation and discipline necessary to succeed in school. Back then I never considered the possibility that the tracking of these students, the curriculum and grading approaches used by teachers, and the teacher-student relationship could be contributing to the "underachievement" of these students.

After 14 years of teaching, I decided to enter a doctoral program at UC Berkeley. I hoped to learn about various theories of motivation and learning that would help me understand and better serve my students. In graduate school, I was drawn to courses and research projects that focused on "underachieving" students of whom the largest percentage always happened to be from the inner city and African American. The literature that I read, written by African American and other scholars, presented me with a completely different way of thinking about the poor performance of many of these students (Collins & Tamarkin, 1982; Cummins, 1986; Heath, 1983; MacLeod, 1987; Marshall & Weinstein, 1984; Oakes, 1985; Ogbu & Matute-Bianchi, 1986; Rubin, 1976).

I became more and more concerned and outraged at the way that African American students have historically been set up for failure. I also became somewhat dismayed about how, as a teacher, I had been given the impression over the years that African American students couldn't perform on the same level as White students, and how I had accepted that idea. As part of a research project while in graduate school, I visited urban elementary schools and observed bright, enthusiastic, articulate African American students. I asked myself how it could happen that many of these students with such obvious potential in elementary school would, according to the literature, become "underachievers" in junior high and high school.

Based on the literature I was reading and the experiences I was having in inner-city schools, I began to believe that the strategies and materials used by their teachers—not the students' shortcomings—were the problem. Three years after I started my doctoral program, I decided to go back into the junior high school classroom to work with so-called low achieving African American children, using alternative teaching strategies that I had developed as part of a school-university research project.

The alternative strategies I used were (1) a noncompetitive classroom structure with effort-based grading, (2) multiple performance opportunities, (3) increased responsibility and choice, and (4) validation of cultural heritage. (For a detailed description of my teaching approach, see Teel, DeBruin-Parecki, & Covington, 1998, and Teel & DeBruin-Parecki, 2001.) With the incorporation of these four strategies into specific lessons, the goal of the curriculum was to increase student academic achievement by recognizing and honoring their diverse learning styles, strengths, talents, and interests.

My curriculum incorporated such innovations as students writing pen-pal letters to other students in Namibia and simulation games such as Starpower and Sanga. I also gave my students creative assignments such as book talks—where students would read a book of their choice and later present the story to their classmates—bookmaking, and student-created crossword puzzles that they made up from historical information. In addition, I was open to having visitors in the classroom. For example, Jennifer invited a man from Timbuktu, a Muslim, to the class while we were studying the ancient African empires and Islam.

In short, I wanted to create a classroom environment encouraging individual effort and group cooperation rather than competition and a win/lose scenario. I developed lessons that students could complete successfully either the first time—if they met the standards I expected—or after they revised their work using my feedback to improve what they had done. Grades were determined on an individual basis, irrespective of the amount of time required, taking into consideration cooperation, participation, effort, and quality of work.

Hence, my students' final grades were based on several criteria, including their participation in class discussions (which I no longer avoided), their performance on a variety of assignments, both traditional and more innovative, and their efforts during role-plays and simulation games. Because of this grading approach, my students' grades were typically higher in my class than they had been in their elementary school years and than they were in their other seventh-grade classes. Many of them said they felt more supported and respected in my class than they had in other classes and that they felt I was fair.

Even with all these positive developments with my students, however, there were many occasions when I knew I was not in control and that the rapport between many of my students and myself was not what I wanted. On a regular basis, exchanges between students or between one or more students and me would flare up and become disruptive. Most of the time, I didn't understand what was happening, what caused the disruption, or how to handle it. It seemed as though my reactions often escalated the conflict, even though that was the last thing I wanted.

I talked about these dilemmas with my colleagues from graduate school, who often had observed the disruptions. At first, we attributed the problems to a flawed curriculum. We considered ways to modify the lesson designs in order to prevent such disruptions the next time. Sometimes, lessons would go extremely well, but the student behavior problems persisted.

A colleague from Berkeley suggested that I visit African American teachers whom she had been observing that year. She told me that she was very impressed with the respectful rapport they had promoted and the businesslike yet very supportive learning environments they had created in their classrooms, which appeared to be very effective. She suggested that I observe Jennifer at our school, where she was currently teaching a group of students who had been removed from their mainstream classes because of continual problems with their teachers. She told me that Jennifer was an example of the kind of effective teacher with African American students whom she had been describing. She noted that Jennifer's approach was different from mine.

I observed Jennifer a few times that second semester. I found her to be surprisingly strict as a classroom teacher; she rarely smiled. She did not permit any talking or off-task behavior and sent students out without hesitation on rare occasions if they would not cooperate. She demanded respect as the authority in the classroom and would settle for nothing less. She also had a way of talking to the students and responding to their academic efforts that was respectful, supportive, and encouraging. Her students responded with attention, focus, and apparent learning.

The experience for me in Jennifer's class was most impressive. I realized as I observed the interaction between Jennifer and her students that I lacked the connection and affinity with my students that Jennifer obviously had.

The next year (1992–1993), I took a leave of absence to finish my dissertation. As I coded and analyzed my data in preparation for writing my dissertation, I couldn't help but notice how many incidents of teacher-student dissonance took place in my classroom over the course of both years. Here are some examples:

> The kids were very noisy, and spoke out repeatedly. They were near impossible to control. (9/10/90)

> I am really perplexed about Kenny [all names of districts, schools, and students are pseudonyms]. I like him a lot: he's very bright, talented in writing, reading, speaking, leading, organizing, and can be very cooperative. Lately, though, he acts as if he hates me and is intent on disrupting the class, showing off, and bringing attention to himself. I think I should ignore his behavior, but, I must admit, I may have "had it" with him. I feel sick inside about this and hope Kenny and I can work it out. For a while there I thought we had developed a pretty good relationship. However, ever since he referred to Ms. Baily (a substitute for me) as a "mother fucker" and I sent him out, he has been hostile. (3/9/92)

> Grace said (and then others agreed) that the discussions in class about things going on in the black community resulted in too much rowdiness. Marcia even said that she did not like the class because it was too rowdy. They said students needed training in how to LISTEN to each other. (6/1/92)

I was unsatisfied with the way I handled many key incidents. Reading over all of those data reinforced my growing self-doubts about my effectiveness with my students. During that same year, I had another traumatic experience at the annual conference of the American Educational Research Association in Atlanta. I attended a session about race, class, and gender differences. During the question-and-answer period, an African American educator said that he believed that a good part of the struggle experienced by African American students in schools could be attributed to their interactions with many of their White teachers, who did not choose to teach African American students. He said that many beginning White teachers accepted positions in inner-city schools because those are the only jobs available. He also asserted that even experienced teachers sometimes were teaching in inner-city schools not out of choice but through involuntary transfers due to low seniority. The educator stated that this situation had to be detrimental to the achievement of African American students, since these White teachers were teaching them involuntarily.

I approached him at the end of the session and told him about my own situation. I said that I had chosen to work with African American students because I believed in them and wanted them to realize their potential for success. He looked me straight in the eye and responded that such a gesture on my part was quite humanitarian, but even with my good intentions I would never be effective with these students. He told me that the gap between our cultures and socioeconomic levels was far too wide to allow us to relate to or understand each other. There would always be tensions and problems that would serve as obstacles to my students' ability to learn from me.

I was completely devastated. I went to my hotel room and cried for more than an hour. Somehow, as a consequence of that conversation, something snapped inside of me. Although for the most part I still believed that the problems between my students and me had more to do with the teaching strategies, I began to consider race as a problem between us.

As a result of that exchange, coupled with the other experiences I described earlier, I concluded that either I should return to teaching mostly White students (as I had the first 14 years of my career) or that I needed help and guidance from an African American teacher whom I respected and who would be able to see what was wrong with the teaching strategies I had developed. I still had not thought about tackling the issue of race.

When I approached Jennifer about joining me in this journey, I did not articulate my fears, self-doubts, and reservations regarding my effectiveness as a White teacher. In hindsight, I believe that I was in denial about them. However, at Jennifer's insistence, we decided to conduct a study examining the impact of racial and cultural differences on the teacher-student relationship even though I was still almost certain that my strategies, not those differences, were the problem. Thus our journey together began.

FROM DIFFERENT BEGINNINGS TO A COMMON GOAL

As we have shown, our stories were very different in our lives and in how and why we embarked on our teaching careers. When we began our work together, Jennifer had been a classroom teacher for only 2 years, whereas Karen was starting her 17th year of teaching and was known in her district to be an effective teacher of White students.

Surprisingly, these differences in our years of formal teaching experience and curriculum work were never an issue between us. Jennifer's expertise was based on her effectiveness as a teacher of African American students, which Karen had observed for herself. It was the *effectiveness* of

Jennifer's teaching, regardless of the number of years she had spent in the classroom, that Karen sought; this is what we both regarded as "teaching expertise."

Another difference was the variation in our original commitment to teaching in general and to working with African American students in particular. Karen started out teaching to support her husband and his career, although she soon became passionate about her work. When she taught African American students early in her career, she saw working with them largely as a service to the school—not as grounded in her concern about their academic achievement. It was her experience in graduate school that prompted her interest in effectively teaching African American students.

Jennifer had always been interested in the successful academic achievement of Black students, from Barbados to the United States. She identified and empathized with many of the children of color who came into her classrooms because of shared experiences. However, unlike her students who had struggled all their lives as members of a minority group in the United States, Jennifer had grown up in an environment in Barbados where her blackness was not seen as a deficit, and where Black people could reach their highest potential. She felt that through the example of her life she could provide a different conception of what it meant to be Black for her African American students.

Jennifer had recognized her African American students' hesitancy in trusting anyone who represented the societal power structure that they believed did not support their best interests. Thus, as she noted earlier, the authority vested by society in her role as a teacher was insufficient as a marker for the effective teaching of these students.

Finally, throughout Karen's "herstory," up until her experiences in graduate school, are narratives of conformism: as a child in Fresno, as an undergraduate at UC Berkeley, and as a beginning teacher, when she did not question the reality that primarily African American children at her junior high school were placed in the lowest tracks while primarily White students were placed in the gifted tracks.

In contrast, Jennifer had resisted society's norms that implied her lack of intelligence, had low expectations for her academic achievement, and limited her potential and full participation as a citizen of the United States. We realized from the start that our lives had been very different. In some ways, the work we've done together is a history of Karen finally becoming a rebel.

CHAPTER 3

Critical Moments in Teacher Research

I'm doing what I feel is my best and I'm still criticized. Yet even though it's my best, I know it's not really my best. It's my best right now. But I know I can be better. It's still hard to hear criticism because I'm trying so hard.

—Karen

I have things to say to you and I don't want to hurt your feelings, but I want to make my feelings known. I want us to establish with each other that it's safe for us to talk even about the hard things. For me to say how I feel, and for you to reply. Even if it gets heated, it's okay.

—Jennifer

IN THIS CHAPTER, we describe the challenges of "going the distance" in this research: the ways we showed our commitment to this collaboration even when our different perspectives clashed time after time. In the midst of the research processes and classroom interactions and negotiating the difficulties of our mentoring relationship, there were pivotal moments in which we each decided whether to continue our work together. As will be shown, a major theme of going the distance in this collaboration was trust—trusting each other and trusting the process we were going through together.

We decided at the beginning of this study that Jennifer would observe Karen and her students, record her observations, and then discuss them with Karen (see the appendix for a more detailed description of the research process and methods). We chose an "active" mentoring relationship between us whereby Jennifer actually sat in Karen's class sessions, instead of a "reflective" relationship in which we might have met on a regular basis outside of the classroom to discuss Karen's perceptions of what happened. We have come to believe that this active mentoring, inside the classroom while teaching is taking place, is essential for struggling teachers to truly come to understand the problematic aspects of their teaching.

CONFLICTING COMMUNICATION STYLES: THE STUDENT QUESTIONNAIRE

Early in the study we administered a questionnaire to the students to get their feedback about the class and to compare these early perceptions with students' perceptions later on. Jennifer describes how she initially developed the instrument and then gave it to Karen for her input.

JENNIFER

Karen suggested that we create a questionnaire that asked the students what teacher characteristics are most important (desirable) to them and if, how, and where race enters into the equation. I also wanted to ask the students if they thought *Karen* was a good teacher and what kind of disciplinarian they thought *she* was. From the start of my visits to Karen's classroom, I observed her seeming lack of control of the classroom environment:

> 5th period, 10:42 a.m.: 25 students present. One AA female is combing her hair. AA male burps out loud. Students around him loudly express disgust. Karen either ignores behavior or does not notice. AA male: "Ms. Teel, can you hurry up and grade my quizzes and tests?" Karen: "I will as soon as I can." Same AA male who burps stands out of his seat and talks to another student. Two AA males are talking loudly across the room to each other. Mr. L (an aide from the classroom next door) walks in, passes Karen, goes to the chalkboard and picks up a piece of chalk. Karen looks over at him. She hadn't noticed when he entered the classroom. He shows her the chalk after he picks it up, and walks back out of the classroom. Karen: "I'm waiting for everyone's eyes on me." [My opinion: An issue of teacher control in her classroom. Whose house is it?] (10/3/93)

It seemed that Karen had a difficult time controlling the students' movements throughout the class period. There was an agenda on the board (see appendix for an example of the daily agenda), but the students manipulated the agenda with talk and actions that slowed down and, occasionally, thwarted this agenda. I recorded more of these types of observations as the weeks went by. As such, when Karen suggested the questionnaire, I wanted to know how the students perceived Karen's control of the class.

I developed a questionnaire that focused on how students thought of Karen as a teacher, as much as it focused on how they thought her being White affected their responses to her in the classroom. Some of the questions explicitly asked students about their reactions to Karen as a White teacher—that is, did the fact that she was White affect the way they learned in class; did students think that White teachers treated them differently from teachers of other races, and so forth. Pertaining to classroom control, students were asked whether or not they liked the way that Karen handled discipline.

The questionnaire was three pages long. The first page was a list of 21 questions that students had to agree or disagree with by answering yes or no. Statements such as the following were included:

> Mrs. Teel helps students who are having difficulty.
> Mrs. Teel is open to suggestions for improving the class.
> She enjoys being with her students.
> She only calls my house to complain about me.
> Students get points for behavior even when they don't deserve them.
> She does not control the class.
> Mrs. Teel is a very good teacher.
> I like Mrs. Teel.

The other two pages contained seven open-ended questions that asked students whether they liked specific aspects of the class (such as the reading time, the seating arrangement, etc.).

Karen was quite resistant to what she felt were some unnecessarily personal questions that I was proposing we include in the questionnaire. She seemed to honestly want to know how the students were responding to her teaching, but she was clearly nervous about what they might say. However, rather than express her discomfort, Karen hid these feelings by questioning the relevance of such questions. She kept asking me, "What do these [questions] have to do with the research?" I replied that it would be good to know the students' opinions about aspects of classroom activities and their feelings toward her as their teacher, as well as their perspectives of her as a White teacher.

I convinced her to trust me on administering the questionnaire with these questions included, even though she kept asking in different ways, "What does this have to do with the research?" I kept answering that question, although I knew it wasn't her *real* question—one that dealt more with her feelings about getting such feedback from the students. I perceived Karen's avoidance of the issue that was really bothering her as an example of similar interactions I'd had with other White people in the past, where what they were saying wasn't really what they were feeling.

In past instances when I experienced this sensation of carrying on two conversations simultaneously, I would try to negotiate both of them. It would take real effort on my part to respond to the unstated feelings—because I could be guessing wrongly what those feelings were, and I'd only find that out in the way that my response was received. Then in the event that I guessed wrong, depending on how important the particular interaction was, to my career for example, I would have to be quick on my feet to find a new and improvised response.

However, in my interactions with Karen I did not feel threatened by her in any way during that early stage of our collaboration (although those feelings did occur later, as I will discuss in another chapter). Still, I was becoming frustrated and angry with her because of all the effort that we were making to have a conversation that really wasn't relevant to the real issue at hand (Karen's discomfort). We could have been spending this time responding to an honest statement from her such as "I really don't know how I feel about such feedback from the students." I knew that I would confront her about it at some point. That point came on November 10, 1993, right after we administered the questionnaire.

The students had left for the day and we were in her classroom together.

Karen exhaled and said, "Boy that was hard!"

I said, "What was?"

She replied, "Doing that questionnaire. It's hard to get feedback like that."

I countered, "So why didn't you say that to me?"

She replied, "Well, I talked to my husband about it and to [a professor at UC Berkeley]."

I shot back, "You should have mentioned it to me! I'm in here with you! Not your husband! Not your professor! We're supposed to be working together. You won't tell me what's really bothering you, but you tell them!"

We argued for some time, and I eventually stormed out of the classroom as tears of anger rolled down my face. I left Karen also crying in the classroom. I went up to the main building and ran into another teacher at the school who, ironically, had been one of Karen's previous students early in Karen's career. We sat on the back stairway, and I told her what had happened. That conversation with her was the moment when I started to say, "Forget this." This emotional turmoil was not worth it. Karen was not worth it. The teacher I talked to also felt that if Karen and I could not develop a relationship of trust perhaps we should not work together. I agreed. I left school that day thinking that the study was over.

However, a few days later we talked on the phone. Karen had called, and we agreed to have lunch together to discuss what had occurred and how we would proceed. As we taped our conversation at lunch, we both recognized this as an important moment in the study. Words in brackets are added to the recorded statements to clarify the dialogue:

> JENNIFER: Karen, after we spoke earlier on the phone, I hung up thinking that I have things to say to you and I don't want to hurt your feelings, but I want to make my feelings known. So, I want us to establish with each other that it's safe for us to talk even about the hard things. For me to say how I feel and for you to reply. Even if it gets heated, it's okay.
>
> KAREN: Yeah, I agree and I also want to be sure that you understand that sometimes I can't verbalize how I am feeling. I don't always know why I'm upset sometimes. I can't always figure it out.
>
> JENNIFER: Why?
>
> KAREN: I'm just not clear what the source is. I'm not clear what's bothering me. I can be helped to understand it, just by kind of talking it out.
>
> JENNIFER: That's good for me to know, because I'm not like that. I immediately know what's bothering me. That's why I really resented you last week because I thought that you knew what was bothering you, and you didn't tell me, but you told other people. What I need for you to do is when there's something happening and you don't understand, say to me "Jen, I'm feeling uncomfortable." Name it, name the emotion. You know what I mean?
>
> KAREN: Okay. Even if I don't know what's coming.
>
> JENNIFER: Right. Say something like, "I don't know where this is coming from, can we talk about it?" So that as we talk it through, we pay attention to our emotions as a way to find out how the experience of whatever we're doing is affecting us. You know what I mean?

KAREN: Yes.

JENNIFER: Because, I remember when you were objecting to the questionnaire, you kept saying that you didn't know what it had to do with this study. And I felt that you really wanted to say that you were feeling uncomfortable about it, period.

KAREN: Yes.

JENNIFER: And I'm like [I said to myself] "I'm not about to guess her feelings. She has to tell them to me." And if you don't tell me your feelings, that's when I get upset.

KAREN: But, those questions. It was the first set about me—all the things about me. The questions I'm talking about are, "Ms. Teel explains stuff well, and Ms. Teel does this, does that," just me as a teacher. Just being singled out, focused on and direct, having them give their opinion. I think part of it was that I have a kind of expectation or hope. Some of it is based on experience and some based on a certain amount of expectation I have of myself, that over the year, the relationship [between the students] and me is going to get stronger. That I'm going to be able to get across to them what I'm trying to do and what I think of them and why I'm there and all that kind of stuff. And why I'm doing what I'm doing in terms of the curriculum and grading and all that. But I don't think that they're there yet.

So, it's just hard, it's hard for me to take the . . . [criticism]. Give it 3 months. I have a hard time with criticism. I feel vulnerable in that particular area. And then to get criticized by my students.

The other thing is, I'm doing what I feel is my best, and I'm still [criticized]. [Yet] even though it's my best, I know it's not really my best. It's my best right now. But I know I can be better. It's still hard to hear criticism because I'm trying so hard.

I can take criticism if I feel like I'm going to learn from it or I'm going to improve from it, but it's hard, and this questionnaire was really helpful. In some ways it was really very encouraging. I mean, very complimentary, but it's still hard. I knew that I would get some negative feedback.

JENNIFER: Had we had this conversation, I would have been there for you. I would have known when to be there for you. We could have connected on the fact that you were really nervous. I was still guessing whether you were nervous or not. And then to hear all of that stuff come out after.

KAREN: It's just so sensitive.

JENNIFER: I know, but to me, the way to get through the sensitivity is to be able to name it, and not necessarily to say why. We may not know why.

KAREN: Right, just say it.

JENNIFER: Just say it. Just say, "Jen, I have to let you know that today is going to be hard for me, I don't know why yet, we can talk about why later." Immediately, I would not be that mean to you. I'm not that much of an ogre. I would have responded with, "How can we make this easier?" And that's another way that our friendship can start to grow, by my being there for you.

I talked to one of my friends the night of our fight. I said that I was contemplating not doing it [the study] anymore. I remember I told her that I thought you were really racist but it's subconscious. I said that you did lip service to do the right thing, but there are times when it [your racist behavior] occurs. And when I tell you about it, you say that it's not true. So, I feel like I'm fighting something that you can't see. I'm fighting a ghost.

That's what I told her. And she said, "You know, your research isn't about the kids. The kids are secondary. Your research is about White teachers and African American teachers, that a lot of what we learned last Wednesday has to do with why White teachers and African American teachers don't get along."

It's interesting to note that someone else realized the significance of our interactions. At the end of that lunch, Karen and I decided that we both needed to get back in there for ourselves and for the kids.

RESULTS OF THE QUESTIONNAIRE

Fifty students completed the questionnaire. Of the 48 who gave an answer to the question of ethnicity, 32 were African American, 7 were Asian American, 2 were of mixed-race heritage (1 Filipino/Italian student, and 1 Indian/Spanish student), 3 were White American and 4 were Hispanic American students. In all, African American students constituted 64% of the group.

In coding the questions regarding "good teacher" characteristics (e.g., explains things well, helps students, is open to suggestions, and is willing to listen), 75% of the students thought that Karen was a good teacher.

Comments such as the following indicated that those who liked the class (70%) attributed that directly to Karen:

> I like the work, some kids and the teacher and the nice way she talk to people.

> Ms. Teel is a good teacher. She help you learn a lot of things about History.

> I like this class because she is nicer to me than any other teacher in [this school] and she listen to everyone in the classroom.

> She always explain things so that we can get the answer right. And she brings history movies that we can learn about history.

Also in specific reference to Karen, 80% of the students did not think that her being White made a difference to how well they learned. When asked if Karen was different from other White teachers they had had, there were a lot of positive responses about Karen as a nice person:

> Yes, she's a better teacher than other White teachers.

> Yes. Well she is nice and she doesn't give lots of homework. Oh, and she doesn't yell at you for no reason.

> Yes, she gives us PAT [preferred activity time].

> Yes, she is way different than my other teachers.

> Yes, because she is nicer, and she can dress.

> Yes, she doesn't act prejudice and she doesn't act rude.

When asked if they thought that African American teachers taught better than White teachers the majority of students said no (70%). These students basically agreed that "sometimes teachers are just teachers. They can teach the same things and they can both be mean or good." Another student was very explicit: "No, it don't matter what color the teacher is. I have 5 White teachers and one Black, and they all teach the same." Overall,

- 73% of the students said that they would not prefer a teacher from their own race;
- 88% of the students were comfortable with White teachers; and
- 90% of the students did not think that White teachers treated them differently from teachers of other races.

The discrepancy in students' responses was on the issue of discipline. A larger percentage of the students in the fifth-period class (60%) than in the third-period class (43%) felt that Karen could not control the class. Students' comments about Karen's lack of classroom discipline were

I hate this class. She does not know how to control it. People are fighting, hitting, and teasing.

She gives warnings but she lets kids get away easy.

She is soft and other teachers make learning more fun.

The noise in the class is too loud.

She don't know how to handle the kids.

She might be afraid of them.

She's too nice to the bad students.

She uses a stop-watch—stupid—(that is very White).

If she was a Black person and those kids started acting stupid like they do, they [the Black person] would have taken control.

She's not in control of the class.

KAREN

The students agreed with Jennifer that I had weak control of the class. Some students said they thought that I was afraid of them. One White student even said that I had no backbone and that my class was not taken seriously. Obviously, the negative responses by my students were devastating to me and dealt me a hard blow. Never before had I been criticized by my students. Of course, I had never administered such a provocative questionnaire before either. I had to decide then whether I could persevere in the study, confronting my shortcomings and trying to overcome them.

My perception of Jennifer as a mentor and collaborator evolved in stages over the first year of our study. I don't think either of us would say that we were friends in the early stages. As I remember, Jennifer and I were strictly colleagues. We agreed that we had common concerns about the academic achievement of African American students and that we might gain some insights into that issue by studying me as a White teacher with my African American students.

At first, I don't think either of us was sure about the other's motives, but we had enough basic trust and commitment to the students to go ahead with this research. In terms of my goals for this research (wanting to improve my teaching), the most important reason for my desire to work with Jennifer was her success as a teacher with this same student population. Without that respect for Jennifer as a classroom teacher, I never would have agreed to engage in this kind of self-scrutiny with her.

However, I hadn't talked to Jennifer about my worries and fears. At that time, I saw our relationship as a professional one in which we were both researchers, conducting a study, attempting to understand the nature of the problem between me and my African American students.

Additionally, I was resisting the vulnerable-teacher image that I now consider a prerequisite for teacher change. I still wanted to believe that I was an excellent teacher—skilled and knowledgeable and with many memories of successful classroom experiences. It was very hard for me to look at myself critically, especially in the company of someone such as Jennifer, whom I respected. I was very nervous about exposing (and especially admitting) to her my shortcomings as a teacher, since our initial relationship had been one of fellow graduate students, and I had just completed my doctoral degree. I felt an aura of confidence in some ways and yet had deep-seated fears about my possible ineffectiveness as a classroom teacher.

My confidence in myself as a teacher (which was still strong, though weakened) and my determination to become a better teacher for my students led me to the decision to continue the study. I believed that Jennifer was having a tough time herself, coming to terms with the problems she was observing in my classroom between my students and me.

Because of the results of the questionnaire, I once again saw Jennifer as a reliable mentor who was clearly in tune with the students' perceptions, whereas I was not. I hadn't realized until then that Jennifer was describing the classroom experience from the students' point of view. The students complained about the exact same things that Jennifer had been pointing out to me. I started to pay attention to her suggestions for changes in my approach. She and I began working out different strategies that I could try out to more effectively "keep the class in check," as described by the kids.

We started truly to collaborate for the first time. I took to heart what she said and wrote, and I struggled to make the changes she was suggesting, even though I wasn't confident that they would succeed. As the research progressed, however, based on the observation notes that Jennifer continued to record, I started again to question her perspective.

NEGOTIATING THE MENTORING RELATIONSHIP

KAREN

As the study progressed in the months following the administering of the questionnaire, I found Jennifer's comments to be mostly critical. They also sometimes felt overbearing. She seemed to defend the students in just about every situation when there was tension between me and one or more of them. She always had questions for me about how and why I handled classroom experiences the way I did and had very few positive observations for me. To be honest, part of me suspected that Jennifer was taking the students' side because, like them, she is African American. I began to wonder if she felt obliged to defend their behavior and to criticize mine, thereby undermining me *because I am White*—not because she really was critical of me. I became discouraged at first and then I got angry. I started to argue with Jennifer in my write-ups. She substituted for me one day, early in the second quarter, and part of the notes for that day read:

> 3rd period: I think the students try to get away with too much with Karen. It annoys me that every time I'm in there, the back row with Crystal, Michael and the other girl talk and giggle throughout the whole period, and most of the time totally ignore Karen's reprimands. (1/11/94)

I replied to Jennifer,

> I find your descriptions of some of period 3's students' behaviors to be exaggerated. I just don't agree with your observations! I know this happens now and then, but you make it sound as if it is going on non-stop all period long. Why don't you document these behaviors more systematically, jotting down the exact time when

each of them takes place. That would help me to accept your descriptions better! (1/18/94)

I attempted to defend my position and my perspective about what happened in class in contrast to Jennifer's point of view. Jennifer wrote:

The kids are noisy. Karen is at her desk but she's not saying anything about the noise. (1/25/94)

I replied:

You wrote that it was noisy after the bell had rung, and students were passing materials out. I was at my desk and didn't comment on the noise. WHAT DO YOU THINK THE PROBLEM IS? I guess I wasn't particularly bothered by the noise. This is the students' first five minutes when they can chat, get organized, talk to me, etc. What do you think the noise level should be under those circumstances? (2/8/94)

My frustration with what I perceived as her overly critical notes was becoming evident, as seen even more clearly in the following example of her notes (each new paragraph represents a different excerpt from the field notes that day), and my responses:

The class goes about the task of getting a book to read during reading time. Karen, "You need your book or get 2 of them if you're not sure." AA female student says to Karen, "Why all your books bunk?" Karen: "Well, you have a big selection or you can bring a book from home." Student walks away.

Karen gets helpers to pass out the folders and homework for the week. There are a lot of exclamations when students see their grades: AA male: "I got a C!" AA female: "Why you gon' give me C?" AA female: "A C!" Karen tries to quiet the class: "Everyone your grade is dropping [she's referring to the daily class behavioral grade]. I see people who are not doing what they're supposed to do." Karen is shouting to get the kids' attention: "This is taking too long. We're right at a C right now and dropping. I'm not getting the responses I need." She pauses, and then says, "Okay, dropping to a D. I'm going to give you guys a D today." AA female student: "A D!" Karen: "Nobody's listening!" AA female yells to the class: "Shut up!" and then tells Karen, "Why don't you start sending them to the time out room?" Karen, "Because there's too many." [My opinion: This is not the answer I would have given. This is a clear example of at least one student seeing Karen as so out of control of the class that she's making suggestions to Karen on how to rectify the situation. I personally would have started to send 1 or 2 kids out. I know that they would protest that they were not doing anything or that everyone was doing something, but my response would have been, "I don't want to talk about it. Until there's quiet in here I'll send out whomever I think is causing disruption."]

Karen diligently continues with her agenda. Karen gets AA male to cooperate by telling him that if everyone is working on his or her assignment, the class grade of D– would go up. The class finally quiets down for the first time during the entire period. (2/1/94)

I responded to Jennifer:

Toward the end of that second page [of your write-up], you write that "the class finally quiets down for the first time during the entire period." I don't agree with your descriptions of the class that period at all. For at least half of the class (beginning, reading time, and discussion of study hall), the students were well behaved and on task. I think your descriptions are a major exaggeration. (2/8/94)

At that point Jennifer started to comment on the terseness of my responses. She wrote to me:

I hope my responses do not appear antagonistic. I felt irritated in some instances when I read your responses to my field notes, like when you write "grossly exaggerated" [among other comments]. It makes me feel as though you doubt my competence. I don't write my observations to put you on the defensive, so it bothers me when I feel that you take them that way. (2/12/94)

The tension between us was again on the rise. Jennifer was becoming annoyed by the tone of my responses, and as my responses indicated, I was already angry. These notes exemplify how negotiation about our points of view regarding what took place in the classroom repeatedly occurred even after we thought that we had made headway in effectively communicating with each other and working together. Overall, this was one of the major difficulties in establishing a mentoring relationship between us. An unexpectedly high rate of criticism from Jennifer, coupled with my perceptions of a racial bias that Jennifer might have had against me, made it difficult for me to accept Jennifer as a mentor.

JENNIFER

In summary, there were many tense moments between Karen and myself, but out of them developed the trust and mutual respect she and I now hold toward each other. I am convinced that the trust and mutual respect in our present relationship could not have developed without these types of moments, even though, at the time of interaction, the moments were experienced as emotionally difficult. These were the moments when it became obvious to us just how much the lives of Americans are impacted by race as a social construct. Recall, for example, Karen's perception of me as being racially biased, some of the students' comments about White and African American teachers, and my race-based perceptions of Karen. Were it not for our stated goal of students' successful academic achievement, many times Karen and I would have packed it in and retreated to our separate lives. However, we developed a mentoring relationship that worked for both of us. Making the classroom a better learning environment for the students became our impetus for entering discomfort zones, and we survived.

CHAPTER 4

Racial and Cultural Perspectives on Student Behavior

I reacted to my African American students based on what I had been taught. I warned students on a regular basis, called home if they did not respond, and sometimes sent them out of the classroom on a referral. I rarely asked the students for an explanation of their behavior and rarely thought about what was causing their "unacceptable behavior."

—Karen

It becomes easy for White teachers to eventually give up and say that the students are incapable of being managed or taught. And partly because of prevalent views of these students as failures, the White teacher is not reprimanded for giving up, but rewarded for even attempting to try in the first place.

—Jennifer

AS TEACHERS, our different expectations of students' behavior and teacher authority were among the biggest challenges we faced in this study. As we've mentioned earlier, we knew that these differences between Karen and her students might interfere with her attempts at forming a positive relationship with them. However, we did not anticipate how important these notions would be in the evolution of our relationship as classroom collaborators.

EXPECTATIONS

In the section below, Karen describes her expectations for student behavior in her classroom and the "cross-cultural disorientation" she experienced when she first started working with inner-city African American students.

KAREN

When I first started teaching at this middle school, I had very rigid views about how students should behave in my classroom and how they should communicate with me. I expected my students to

1. automatically pay attention to me when I talked;
2. listen to one another;
3. sit quietly in their seats when being spoken to;
4. raise their hands when they wanted to say something;
5. speak standard English;
6. speak politely;
7. follow my directions without complaint; and
8. show respect toward me as the teacher.

I had been told in my teacher education program and in my first teaching position that these were desirable classroom behaviors fostered by an effective classroom teacher. I was also encouraged to demand these kinds of behaviors and to follow through with clear consequences if the students did not conform to these expectations. Throughout my many years of teaching mostly middle-class White students, these precepts had seemed to serve well in establishing a classroom environment that supported delivery of the substantive curriculum.

In "Silencing in Public Schools," Fine (1987) described the way this kind of criteria for successful teaching of African American students is justified by White teachers. She wrote that the unofficial school policy has to do with protecting the students from "facing themselves," wanting them to learn what they must learn in order "to succeed" in middle-class, White America. Behaving in class means conforming, being quiet, and not creating controversy. Differences of opinion boldly expressed indicate lack of discipline and weak control.

I am not certain how typical I am as a veteran middle-class White teacher, but I assumed that my primarily inner-city African American students needed more guidance in how to behave. For the first few years that I worked with these students at the middle school, I struggled because of the differences in attitudes and behavior between them and myself. Even though my students' grades were often better than they had been in the past because of the innovative curriculum and grading approaches I was using, I found that many of my students had characteristics that I was not used to and wasn't sure how to handle. Some examples of this behavior were what I perceived as

1. an aggressive communicative style;
2. unfamiliar expressions;
3. the need to save face in front of peers;
4. a demand for respect from peers and the teacher;
5. vocal and honest expressions of dissatisfaction with the class; and
6. a tendency to test me as a person of authority.

In my notes to Jennifer I describe some of the problems I was having with both my third- and fifth-period classes:

I seem to have trouble every day getting the students in period 3 to listen when we go from one activity to another. Certain students seem oblivious to my requests for quiet. I have had to use the stopwatch a number of times to remind them of the importance of class time for working and not wasting time. The time accumulated on the stopwatch is taken off their P.A.T. (Preferred Activity Time) on Friday. I also have the problem of students getting out of their seat without permission. I don't enforce that rule as consistently as I should.

There are several "problem" students in this 5th period class as compared to 3rd period. They appear to be more resistant, angrier students. They find every excuse to complain, find fault with what I do or ask them to do. They are very chatty and bring experiences from lunch or the day before etc. with them into my classroom. Sometimes, we will be discussing a topic and suddenly, often unexpectedly to me, several students will break into smaller conversations or will just begin their own private conversation. I often ask for quiet and then pull out the stopwatch. I have called the homes of these problem students a number of times. (9/20/93)

In effect, I reacted to my African American students based on what I had been taught. I warned students on a regular basis, called home if they did not respond, and sometimes sent them out of the classroom on a referral. I rarely asked the students for an explanation for their behavior and rarely thought about what was causing their "unacceptable behavior."

However, Jennifer came into my classroom and had quite a different reaction to my students' behavior, as well as to my responses to their behavior. The following vignette, written from Jennifer's perspective, is an example of a classroom incident in which she and I perceived student disruption very differently. We call this incident "Why You Call Me a Barbarian?"

"WHY YOU CALL ME A BARBARIAN?" Jennifer describes this incident as follows:

A lesson Karen conducted with her 3rd period class didn't work well much to her surprise and frustration. She and a colleague had prepared a reading on 6 groups who lived during the time of the Roman Empire and what their individual problems were as the empire was collapsing. They had prepared an accompanying chart on which the students were to write in their own words what each group's problems were based on the reading. In order to promote the historical thinking concepts of empathy and multiple perspectives, each student would be assigned to one of the 6 groups. The roles were: Barbarians, Common people/Farmers, Emperors, Nobles, Soldiers, and Gladiators/Slaves. Karen assigned the roles to the kids:

Tolanda demands: "What you give me common people for?"

Karen answers: "I'm just going down the roll. Sam, you're a barbarian, so to speak."

Another student responds: "What's all this slave and barbarian?!" The kids appear very agitated.

Karen: "I don't like this talking. I want it to stop now."

There were a few bright moments during the lesson. For instance, Sam explained the struggles of the barbarians brilliantly by asserting that the Romans were prejudiced against them—just because they looked different and behaved differently. Roy responded to Sam with: "Where does it say that?" Karen explained that Sam had taken the information and come up with an analysis or further interpretation of it. After she explained Sam's analysis to Roy, Sam demanded: "So why you call me a barbarian?" In that moment, Karen's explanation further indicted her as insulting the student. She had praised Sam's interpretation of how barbarians were viewed by the Romans right after calling him one during the role-play. (10/20/93)

There was an intense discussion between us during the lunch break about what had taken place earlier in the classroom. I told her that I had had similar problems in the past when I assigned roles. Jennifer responded that she thought the kids found the roles insulting. I replied that I thought that if I did the activity again it would go very well because the students might not be so anxious. Jennifer pointed out to me that the students' responses might sometimes be more than disruption or "attitude." Sometimes, talking back is their only way of conveying problems they may have with the content of the lesson.

Apparently, my approach to the lesson lacked sensitivity to my students' racial and cultural identities. In my approach to the role-play, I did not say, "Student, you read the role of barbarian." Jennifer suggested that this mode of presentation would have put some distance between the students and the role itself. As she explained, for me to say, "Sam, you're a barbarian" did not distinguish the distance existing between the student's identity and the role-play.

Moreover, although I admitted that I had received similar responses from students in the past, it still had not occurred to me that the activity might be the problem. I was convinced of the "rightness" of the activity because a colleague and I had taken time to prepare it with the students' best interests in mind. Our efforts were based on enabling students to understand better and become more engaged in the lesson. Role-playing, then, was a way of adhering to advice from the educational literature encouraging teachers to make lessons more interactive.

BLAMING THE STUDENTS. How could such a strategy go wrong? When students' responses did not follow expectations, I shifted the blame: It was the students' fault. I thought that the students reacted the way they did because they weren't mature enough to handle that kind of role-playing or that the roles seemed totally remote and silly to them. I never thought that the students would be offended by being given the role of barbarian or slave—and yet Jennifer picked right up on that. We each had a totally different perspective.

As I reflected after our conversation, I wondered how many other times students had been offended by the assignment and I had seen their behavior only as students "acting up." In my mind, I was clearly separating my students as students and my students as African Americans whose ancestors had experienced the horrific event of American history known as slavery. I did not relate to my Whiteness in terms of the symbolic representation of me as a White woman calling a student who is Black a slave.

I thought the students would think that the role-playing was fun, like playing a game. I never expected this approach to insult them. I have been trying to think through and explain how I could have been so oblivious to my students' feelings, which come from their history of slavery and oppression in this country. I think that since I grew up without that personal history on my mind, it didn't occur to me that this role-playing might be offensive. Also, I did not anticipate that my middle school students from the inner city would have those kinds of feelings.

Was that racist? Is "White privilege" an example of racism? (Edwards, 1998; McCarthy & Crichlow, 1993; McIntosh, 1989). McIntosh (1989) refers to "white privilege" as an "invisible knapsack." She states: "I have come to see white privilege as an invisible package of unearned assets which I can count on cashing in each day, but about which I was 'meant' to remain oblivious" (pp. 10–12). When I refer to "white privilege" and racism, I am thinking that since I grew up believing that my issues—White, middle-class issues—were the most important issues, that I wasn't able to see the potential response of my students to one of their issues, an African American issue, of the legacy of slavery.

I'm saying that such preconceived notions about what my students will or won't feel are both examples of "white privilege" and of a racist attitude on my part, unconscious but very real (Hollins & Spencer, 1990; Ladson-Billings, 1996; King & Ladson-Billings, 1990; Steele, 1992). This may be another example of the "ghost of racism." Hanssen (1998) comments on the subtleties of institutional racism:

> We need to remember that institutional racism typically isn't ugly. Rather than being expressed through racial slurs, it tends to be wrapped in noble proclamations of tradition, fairness, and high standards. Rather than being a rare incident, it is woven into the fabric of our historically racist society. (p. 698)

All of what occurred in the incident discussed earlier may not have been a result of racism, but if any aspect of my behavior reflected the institutional racism described by Hanssen, then I felt it imperative that I ferret out these aspects and attend to them.

One aspect of classroom dynamics became very clear to me as a result of the incident, however. That is, it seems more likely that teachers will blame students for unacceptable behavior in the class rather than reflect on how a class activity or the teacher's own behavior might be helping to produce the unacceptable behavior. Teachers should be sensitive to this tendency to blame students and continue to question their own biases and quick assumptions about so-called student disruptions in the class-room.

Another example of an incident in which I was oblivious to cultural differences with my students was when one of them used his "home language" during a discussion. This incident took place during the simulation game Starpower. We are calling that incident "Cause We Raw."

"CAUSE WE RAW." I had the students play this game to give them a feel for the dynamics of power in societies where there are different classes. I wanted the students to be able to identify with people in the various groups so that when we studied feudal societies (such as those that existed in Europe, Japan, Africa, and China) they would hopefully have an easier time grasping these hierarchies.

During the game, as a result of a few bargaining sessions with chips, the students ended up in one of three hierarchical groups: the Squares (the highest), the Triangles (the middle), or the Circles (the lowest). There were about seven students at each of the three tables. Roy was a member of the Squares, and Deon was a member of the Circles group. At one stage of the game, the student groups of Triangles and Circles were having a very difficult time being perceived as members of obviously disenfranchised groups. This was a particularly difficult time for those students who in the context of "traditional" curricular activities such as question-and-answer assignments and tests were considered A students, and who now—in compliance with the game—were identified with either the Triangles or Circles group. At one point during the game, I asked the Squares to decide on new rules, since their group was the wealthiest and most powerful one. The Squares' second rule read: "Take all of the other kids' scores and add them to the Squares' scores." I asked the spokesperson for the group, Roy, to explain to the class why his group (the top group) had decided to take money from the other two groups in the game for themselves. Here is how Jennifer described the interaction between the students that followed:

> "Cause we raw," says Roy assertively. Deon, a member of the Circles, yells out sarcastically, "Raw fish." Roy returns, "Raw fish with money." Carol, a fellow member of the Squares, states emphatically and in a very proud voice, "I heard that!" (11/17/93)

Throughout this exchange I didn't understand the meanings of the words the students were using, so I acted oblivious. As if the conversation wasn't taking place, I kept asking Roy that same question (Why did the

Squares decide on rule #2?) over and over again so that I would get an answer that made sense to me. Finally, Roy answered: "Cause we got power over them. We want more power over them." (11/17/93)

Jennifer later explained what was happening during the student exchange in her dissertation (Alleyne Johnson [Obidah], 1995a):

> This interplay of language between the students demonstrates use of their "home"—as opposed to "school"—language. In the exchange, a cultural connotation of the word raw referenced the Squares' power and domination over the Triangles and Circles. Deon, the student member of the Circles, skillfully employed the African American oral tradition of signifying in his scathing rejoinder of "raw fish," to Roy's deliberate flaunting of the Squares' power.
>
> Henry Louis Gates Jr. (1984) defines signifying as a mode of discourse arising from African American culture, whose learned concepts are "often part of our adolescent education." Gates quotes Mitchell-Kernan's assertion that the "Black concept of signifying incorporates essentially a folk notion that dictionary entries for words are not always sufficient for interpreting meanings or messages, or that meaning goes beyond such interpretations." Roy, cognizant of this shared cultural ethos and equally confident in this type of discourse described by Gates, replied to Deon's rejoinder of "raw fish" with: "raw fish with money!" Roy's reply demonstrated his keen comprehension of the power of money to elevate even the status of raw fish. Carol's "I heard that!"—the words plus the intonation—validated Roy's statement. (pp. 93–94)

At the end of the class, Jennifer pointed out to me what an opportunity I had missed to learn something from the students about their home language. In "Fighting for Our Lives," Ladson-Billings (1996) writes: "Cultural competence can be supported in the classroom by acknowledging the legitimacy of students' home language and using it as a bridge to edited English" (p. 12). Along those lines, Jennifer told me that the fact that the students were using their home language indicated to her that they were engaged in the activity and feeling very comfortable with me.

Truthfully, I was nervous about admitting my ignorance of such expressions and about putting Roy in what I thought would be an awkward position where he had to explain himself—putting him in a way on the defensive. I was so amazed when Jennifer told me what he was saying and what it meant because I was sure he was saying something else such as "wrong" or "robbed." I don't know why I didn't ask him to explain what he was saying.

Sometimes, my African American students—both this year and in previous years—have become frustrated with me when I haven't understood them, as if they feel inept when they are not understood. Or they just may be tired of their teachers not understanding them because the teachers have no experience with their students' language outside of school. Or the students feel as though I in particular am embarrassing them—maybe on purpose.

At any rate, having had such reactions to my requests for language clarification, I guess I tended to hesitate to ask students directly about their language use when I couldn't understand them. I felt ignorant and uncomfortable myself when I didn't understand and was embarrassed to ask. Jennifer convinced me to disregard such fears, because it can be so validating to the students when I show genuine interest in their different uses of language and indicate to them that they also can teach me.

The most disturbing aspect of these incidents in my classroom was my complete oblivion when they occurred. If it hadn't been for Jennifer, to this day I would not understand why each of those situations was problematic. These are examples of how a White teacher in an urban school sabotaged her own good intentions through ignorance of racial and cultural differences and possibly through unconscious racist notions about the students. Uncovering these problematic characteristics was one of my greatest fears but something that I knew I had to do.

CHANGING EXPECTATIONS. As a result of my collaboration with Jennifer during the first year of our study, I changed dramatically in the way I thought about my students and the way I dealt with them. The relationship I had with my students improved substantially. I began to understand that the students' behavior was not necessarily defiant just because it was not what I expected, but represented a different, yet equally valid, way of communicating and interacting:

1. I began to listen to my students—when they expressed anger and frustration with me, with another student, or with the subject matter—instead of reacting in a negative way.
2. I redefined inappropriate behavior so that at times I would interpret disruptions as joint problems that needed to be addressed by the entire class or dealt with privately one on one with the disruptive student.
3. I learned from my collaboration with Jennifer that disruptions can have multiple causes, which call for multiple responses. It was a challenge for me in the 2nd and 3rd years of our collaboration to understand the differences.

As a result of these changes on my part, the students became more respectful toward me as their teacher and more accepting of my authority.

Jennifer's views about what African American students need in school have been validated over and over again through my interactions with my students, which have continued to improve because of my work with her.

JENNIFER

From Karen's early descriptions of her students, her feelings about them were evident. It was very clear that in the beginning of the study, Karen perceived some students as problems that needed solving. First, she analyzed both classes only in terms of the problems that *she* had with the students (e.g., their resisting her requests for quiet). Second, students' undesirable behavior never gave Karen pause for thought in terms of her teaching. Instead, she just asked for quiet as usual. In short, the students' behavior was not what she expected and therefore had to be stopped. However, as time went on, particular incidents in the class demonstrated that perhaps there was more to students' misbehavior than their having an "attitude."

In the incidents that we named "Why You Call Me a Barbarian?" and "Cause We Raw," initially, Karen's actions were actually working against her own good intentions. As a result, students were demonstrating undesirable (to Karen) behavior, even though their behavior was in direct response to Karen's actions, which did not take into account her students' racial and cultural identities. When this cycle continues unattended to, it becomes easy for the teacher to eventually give up and say that the students are incapable of being managed or taught. And partly because of prevalent views of African American students as failures, the White teacher is patted on the back for trying to achieve a goal with insurmountable odds: that is, educating these students, especially African American students from economically disadvantaged backgrounds. The teacher is not reprimanded for giving up, but rewarded for even attempting to try in the first place. However, there are instances in classrooms when, regardless of racial and cultural differences, teachers should strongly address inappropriate student behavior and assert their authority.

TEACHER AUTHORITY

Teacher authority and student discipline were two of the most consistent issues that we wrestled with over the year. Because of our different perceptions in the beginning, we discussed teacher authority a number of times at great length, and Jennifer describes the challenges of this issue.

JENNIFER

I thought that Karen hadn't been able to establish strong enough authority as the teacher in her classes. She argued that the students would become more cooperative as they experienced more and more success in her class. I disagreed and said that she had to assert her authority and not wait for it to happen through the students' experiences with the curriculum.

At that time, Karen was bent on setting up a democratic classroom where the students would have a strong voice in decisions that were made regarding rules and curriculum. I warned her that because the students were not used to that kind of an approach on the part of the teacher, she may lose more of their respect, hampering her ability to control the class.

In the early part of the study, it was clear that our styles of classroom discipline were very different. Karen often ignored student infractions that occurred. For example, in one set of Karen's notes that were written prior to the period I started my observation, she wrote that "someone sprayed water on the wall. I played it down." In another incident I recorded how students in Karen's class were popping small firecrackers. The popping sound was heard three times during the period. Karen did not refer to the noise. I wondered why, since the noise was so obvious. However, at the end of the class, when only one student remained, Karen asked him about the noise. Later she told me that she had noticed, but because she could not tell who was doing it, she decided not to react. I would have addressed the noise immediately when it occurred, thereby preempting the second and third moments of classroom disruption.

Thus, while Karen was perceived by the kids, in their own words, as "letting them kids run all over her!" they saw me as much stricter. The students often tried to manipulate this discrepancy in Karen's and my teaching styles. For example, when I was observing the class I usually sat in a front corner of the room while Karen usually stood in the front center. If Karen was teaching an activity that students chose not to pay attention to, they would start to complain to me about how boring the activity was or tell of some other reason why they refused to pay attention to Karen.

If I did not respond to what the students were saying, they would then try talking loudly to each other in front of me while ignoring Karen, and they knew—from past experiences when I substituted for Karen— that I would not ignore this behavior if I were the teacher. In fact, they would not have even attempted to behave that way. Since they knew I was a very strict teacher who asserted my authority in reaction to such student behaviors, I felt that they wanted to see if I would do anything to defend Karen's authority as the teacher or assert my own teacher authority and thereby usurp Karen. Karen continually ignored behaviors that were, in effect, opportunities given to her by the students to assert herself as an authority figure who had earned their respect, as opposed to a teacher who expected students' respect without earning it, respect presumed to accompany the role of teacher.

Yes, students' bad behaviors are often opportunities for teachers. It's not as if the students didn't know what they were doing. They did. They wanted to see if *Karen* knew what she was doing regarding disciplining the class as the teacher, and part of knowing what she was doing was to know how to "don't play," that is, how to maintain classroom control regardless of how students chose to test her. In the following pages I detail an example of the students' behavior with Karen one day after I had substituted for a week while Karen was away.

Ms. JOHNSON (OBIDAH) DON'T PLAY! This incident occurred in the 5th period on the day that Karen returned, and the interactions began during lunch. The students told Karen how much fun they had had with me. However, once the lunch period was over and the class period began, the students began to test Karen's authority in very obvious ways. For example, they were unusually loud and talkative, and Karen kept asking them to be quiet. Some of the students were particularly rude, as shown in this exchange between Karen and a student:

> KAREN: "Listen or you're not going to know what to do."
> SAM: "I'm sick of learning about Islam."
> KAREN: "Sam, if you don't want to be in here I'll have to send you out. Alvin, guys we're dropping [referring to the class grade on behavior which was also part of the students' grade]."

> The students continue to be noisy and to ignore Karen's instructions (which was behavior that had not occurred between Karen and this class for some time). Karen, in exasperation, finally writes a referral for one student to the time out [a room staffed by teachers where students are sent as a punishment]. She then addresses the whole class: "I'm getting sick and tired of people being rude. When I talk you should listen because when you talk, hopefully other people and I listen. Marcus! Marcus!! Your eyes should be on your book. Grace, that's a warning to you."

The class was finally quiet, but sullen. I asked Karen if she would mind if I talked to the students, asking them about their behavior in class today. The most vocal students, primarily African

American females, were the ones who initially participated in the discussion. However, as the conversation progressed, Manuel and Alvin started to mock students who were seriously engaged in discussing why the class was different when Karen taught and when I taught. They rudely interrupted Claire's narrative a number of times. Since I was the adult facilitating the discussion, I considered Alvin and Manuel's behavior an affront to my authority. I saw their deliberate rudeness as a test. They were testing to see if I was really any different from Karen, if I could control the class. I could not ignore their behavior, since all the students were observing the outcome.

I put up with their behavior for a minute or so, and then I turned around and looked at them. My tone of voice and easy manner changed abruptly. I walked right up to their desks (in other words, got up in their faces) and I said sternly, "That's enough! I'll give you a referral and send you out of here." Alvin immediately quieted down. Manuel continued for another moment and then he too was quiet. The whole class sensed that my manner had changed.

The expectant silence that momentarily filled the room was broken by Claire, who said, "See, that's what I'm talking about. Ms. Johnson don't play."

Then Linda, another student, said, "It's something else too but it's personal."

Claire said, "just say it."

Linda replied, "No, I ain't gonna say it cause people's feeling would get hurt."

I responded, "As long as it's not disrespectful you can say it."

Claire and a few other kids urged her to say what she wanted to say.

Linda returned, "Okay I'll say it." She paused and I could see that she was still debating whether to say it or not. Then she said, "Part of it is that Ms. Johnson is Black and Ms. Teel is White." No one said anything. Linda became embarrassed and said loudly, "Y'all know it's true."

The class erupted into a discussion. Claire and Grace nodded their heads in agreement. Not all the kids agreed, but those who did were louder in their agreement than those who didn't. The class ended soon after this comment. (12/16/93)

Karen and I talked afterward. I didn't feel race had everything to do with it, but I felt that it had something to do with it. Race comes into play in my relationship with students in that they expect Black teachers not to put up with inappropriate behavior and that the disapproving responses would be swift, so they tend not to test as much. Also, the expectations for me not to be a bad or boring teacher are higher. I believe that they had higher expectations of my being more capable of entertaining them, that is, making learning more exciting, and overall of my teaching them so that they would learn. In addition, they wanted to like me; they wanted to have that sense of solidarity with me that was based on our Black identities. It's not that they will feel this way with me just because I'm Black. I have to be a good teacher first. However, the advantage of their willingness to meet me halfway in terms of building a good relationship means that there's potentially less antagonism from them, which allows my efforts at being a good teacher to go a little more smoothly. But if I am not interesting or if I'm more of a disciplinarian than a teacher, then the edge that being Black gives me becomes a moot point.

STUDENT DISCIPLINE

JENNIFER

Karen's and my discipline tactics were very different. I didn't ignore behaviors as much as Karen did. I also realized that I gauged better than Karen which kids to come down hard on at what moments. Basically if a kid is being very obvious with eating or bad behavior, that's my cue, because I take their behavior as a personal affront, especially when the other students know that I, the teacher, can't help but notice, since it's so obvious.

Interestingly enough, the classroom moment described earlier occurred a week after our conversation about how Karen handles discipline in the class. Karen admitted that she realizes when students are testing her (we were talking about Mitchell acting up in class the whole period), but she doesn't say anything for a while because she's afraid it will cause a rift between her and the students, and she doesn't want that. I replied that I didn't want that either, but I believed that the students had to understand that the teacher had boundaries in terms of respect and that I also had explicit expectations of what was appropriate and inappropriate behavior. To ignore the behavior made it *explicitly unclear* to the students what was acceptable and unacceptable to the teacher.

From our conversation that day, I realized that Karen wasn't "clueless," as I often thought of her with regard to disciplining the students, since she ignored obviously inappropriate student behavior. I learned that, in fact, she was afraid. She was afraid to jeopardize the tenuous relationship of care and mutual respect that she wanted so desperately to develop with these students. I think that was based on a mistaken view of these kids as "different" because they are African Americans.

All children need boundaries. They need guidance from adults about what's at stake in the actions they choose to take in any given context. They need to see that adults can provide guidelines for them, that adults are explicit about what these guidelines are, and about the rationale for asking kids to abide by these guidelines. But Karen didn't provide any such guidelines, because Blackness and Whiteness tempered the interactions and made her forget that the people she was interacting with were just kids. When students are given boundaries and direction, this leads to the development of good teacher-student relationships, not the opposite.

Once I realized that Karen really didn't know how to navigate her genuine care for the students across racial and cultural barriers, it was easier for me to help her. I realized that her instinct about how to respond effectively to the students was warped by her beliefs, though well intentioned, that informed her interactions with her students and, conversely, her students' interactions with her. For example, Karen had certain instincts: instincts to ignore marginally bad behavior, to hesitate when addressing issues about race in front of the students, and to reward students for every little thing they did, as opposed to rewarding student achievements that really merited reward and praise. These instincts were actually working against her goal of establishing mutual respect between herself and her students.

KAREN

As I mentioned earlier in this chapter, I had serious insecurities about the nature of the relationship that I should develop with my students. I was approaching them in a way that made sense to me given my insecurities: assume they will accept you as an authority figure, keep your distance, and, if there are problems, work them out democratically with the students.

As I was working with mostly African American students, I didn't want to cause a rift in our relationship by coming down too hard on any of them, but I also didn't think I should get too close to any students either. Such an approach was the opposite of what the students wanted and needed from me. That is what I learned from their responses on the questionnaire and from Jennifer.

I learned that my students wanted me to establish my authority, to take charge, and, if there were problems, to enforce the rules, send students out, and be in control at all times. They also wanted me to show more interest in them as individuals. On the questionnaire mentioned in the last chapter, and in interviews with Jennifer, the students agreed that only when strict discipline is maintained by a caring teacher will the students respect the teacher and be willing to work at learning the subject matter.

I also believed that my role as the authority figure in the classroom would be enough to command the students' respect. I never considered the possibility that I might be able to develop the kind of dual relationship with my students that I observed them having with Jennifer, in which at times we might be joking around and talking about subjects unrelated to my classroom while at other times—during lessons—there would be more of a businesslike atmosphere in the class. Somehow, for me, the two positions seemed contradictory or incompatible, even though I had seen it work for Jennifer with her own students.

Jennifer and I discussed the issue of teacher authority and how it is an earned status for inner-city African American students as opposed to a given. Just because I am the teacher doesn't mean that they will automatically respect and oblige me. There must be trust as well. That takes time to build, and there must be some reason for them to trust me. With a White teacher, such respect and trust are far from automatic. They must be earned. I had never considered that possibility, but, again, it makes complete sense to me now.

As a result of feedback from Jennifer and the students, I changed my discipline style:

1. I began to assert my authority more clearly and forcefully when I realized that my students expected such a posture from me.
2. I became more demanding in terms of classroom control and academics, assigning after-school work sessions, and calling home on a regular basis as consequences for inappropriate behavior and missing work.
3. I began to look upon my students as "my children" as opposed to "other people's children" (Delpit, 1995). What this means is that I am putting the same kinds of expectations and pressures on my students as I would on my own children, and at the same time, I am treating them with respect and affection.

As a result of these changes on my part, the students became more respectful toward me as their teacher and more accepting of my authority. Both classes ran more smoothly in terms of cooperation than they had earlier in the year. For example, during the reading time students settled down much faster. Every student had a book to read, and some students even started before I gave the instruction to begin. I rarely had to warn individuals or the whole class about behavior problems.

I think there was another issue involved in my approach to my students, which I also described in chapter 2. Being White, I was nervous about getting close to my students because I didn't feel comfortable with my lack of familiarity with the differences between us—such as our home environments, histories, and cultures—and I assumed that they wouldn't be comfortable with a closer relationship with me either. Jennifer encouraged me to break through such racial barriers, to let down my guard when it felt appropriate, and to let the students and me get to know each other as human beings inside as well as outside of the classroom. I found this new way of relating to the students to be a struggle at first because I wasn't accustomed to it, but little by little, I could feel a much healthier relationship developing between us.

It became quite obvious to me as the year progressed—as I worked at changing my approach to meet the needs and expectations of my students—that when I was more "in control," they became more interested and engaged in the assignment than they had been during more chaotic times. They also responded very positively whenever I showed how much I cared about them, both as students in my class and as young people in other facets of their lives. It all makes perfect sense in hindsight, but I so easily could have continued to miss the point!

As a result of thinking of my students differently, I have changed the way I talk to them and work with them. By the end of the first year, Jennifer had commented on those changes that had occurred. She observed that I was more honest about my feelings and that I had responded to students' criticisms of the class by talking to them more about assignments and activities, informing them of my rationale, and sometimes giving them choices about how to proceed.

GAUGING STUDENT RESPONSES

JENNIFER

I became invested in Karen not giving up. So I started informing her on how to read the students' responses differently. For example, I started to teach her about observing students' reactions to other students' behaviors as a way to distinguish when there was a consensus among the students about what behaviors were serious offenses that warranted the teacher's attention. This was the case when students' responses were exhibited to deliberately undermine the teacher's authority or at least make her earn her authority as a "mean" but good teacher. Later, after signs of a genuine relationship of mutual respect were forthcoming from the students toward

Karen, I taught her how to see when the students were just teasing her, pretending to be bad as a way to share a perhaps stern but yet affectionate moment.

After these lessons started to take effect and the relationship between Karen and her students improved, I let her "go for self." That is, I encouraged her to practice what she had learned in terms of the ability to distinguish between the different behaviors of her African American students, behaviors that all had the potential to disrupt the teaching and learning agenda, but all of which could potentially be managed once the teacher had the ability to recognize what each type of behavior meant in terms of her role as teacher. Karen eventually had to learn how to navigate the inevitable stormy interludes as well as the moments of calm in the wave of exchanges with racial and cultural undertones that occurred between her and her African American students. Stormy interludes and moments of calm are found in all genuine relationships, so they should also be an expected part of addressing relationships that struggle with the issues of racial and cultural differences between people. Karen was a good study.

Karen began to interact with the students in a much more respectful way. It could no longer be said that she did not have control of her class. These developments were great for me to witness. I learned about one example of her changing relationships with her African American students during the second half of the year. In one of my write-ups, I asked about Alvin, whom I hadn't seen for some time. In her response to me, Karen wrote:

> Alvin has moved to San Francisco apparently to live with his mother. I will really miss him. Why? Alvin was very difficult to deal with in the beginning of the year in terms of his attitude and behavior. I worked with a particular woman in his group home a number of times, as we thought of ways to help Alvin settle down. Once he settled down, it became apparent that he was an extremely intelligent, articulate young man with a lot to say and contribute. He had become more and more diligent in his work in recent weeks and more polite and cooperative. He had become a delightful person to be around. He also came in at lunch and was fun to talk to. I hate to lose students like Alvin right when I feel that we are coming to respect one another and to care about each other. This is one of my biggest frustrations about working with the kids who move around either within the school or outside the school. I want to be able to continue to build a relationship of trust and mutual respect, and a lot of my energy goes into that effort. I can only hope that the students who have to go will remember what we built together. (1/18/94)

CHAPTER 5

The Risks in Crossing Boundaries

I knew, even given my current beliefs about these students, that, underneath that recently awakened side of me, a racist attitude (leading to racist behavior) might very well exist.

—Karen

As a Black person you ask yourself, "How can I trust someone who thinks, consciously or subconsciously, that something is wrong with me—to the extent that this something (tangible only in terms of physical difference) makes me an inferior human being?"

—Jennifer

IN THIS CHAPTER, we frame our experiences in terms of what we now reflect on as risks that we took, as two teachers—from different racial and cultural backgrounds—investigating the consequences of racial and cultural differences in Karen's classroom. Each of us writes about what we perceived as our own risks along the way, including the ways that we each thought we could be negatively influenced by this collaboration both personally and professionally.

KAREN'S RISKS

When I decided that I needed help in becoming a more effective teacher with my African American students, I did not consider any possible risks for myself personally. I was very concerned about the difficulties I had experienced over the past 2 years in my classroom, and I was certain that, with Jennifer's help, I would modify the curriculum so that it would better serve the needs of my students. At that point, I did not believe that racial and cultural differences between my students and myself were the cause of the problems I was having. However, as Jennifer and I became immersed in the study, I began to realize that my difficulties with my students might have more to do with racial and cultural differences than I had ever imagined. As I mentioned earlier, although this possibility had been suggested to me at various times in recent years, I did not accept such a notion. As our study progressed, I began to recognize that I was indeed taking risks by doing this research and that our work had possible implications not only for what Jennifer, fellow teachers, fellow researchers, my family, and my friends would find out about me and think about me, but also for what I would learn about and then think of myself.

AS A TEACHER

When I began this work with Jennifer, I had decided to look at all of the possible reasons why my work with inner-city African American students was not as effective as my work had been with White, middle-class students. I knew that Jennifer would have the best interests of the students in mind and that they would be her top priority. I knew she would be very frank with me about her impressions. That is exactly what I thought I wanted because I respected Jennifer in a number of ways—her effectiveness as an inner-city classroom teacher and her graduate work at Yale in African American Studies and at UC Berkeley in education.

This respect for Jennifer made me feel especially hopeful that any problems I had with the students could be solved with her help. I was hoping that Jennifer would reassure me about how my teaching was going and that her suggestions would guide me to more effective teaching. At the same time I was somewhat nervous because if she was critical of me I would be more devastated than I would be by an observer for whom I didn't have the same regard. However, I had reached a state of desperation in my efforts to successfully work with this student population. I wanted to continue to teach them despite the dissatisfaction I was feeling about the results so far. I figured that I may as well explore the difficulties I was having so that I could decide whether I could effectively teach these students.

I was confident as a teacher of White, middle-class students, so I knew I could go back to teaching that student population if this journey failed. Still, the prospect of being a less than successful teacher with my

African American students worried me a great deal. Unlike many White teachers I've known, I wouldn't be able to blame the students.

AS A RESEARCHER

As researchers, Jennifer and I carved our path together every step of the way. Right at the beginning of our work, we decided how we would collect and code data. As described in the appendix, we both carefully documented the classroom experience; periodically, we wrote reflective notes; Jennifer administered two questionnaires; and Jennifer conducted informal interviews with the students in both classes.

This situation presented me with a conflict of interests. As a researcher I knew that we should get the students' honest impressions about what was working and what wasn't in terms of my practice. As a teacher, I felt very vulnerable, however, as I considered the possible findings. The risk here was of setting myself up for failure. This is the double-edged sword of teacher research. If you don't study yourself, you will not learn the aspects of your practice that need to be improved. On the other hand, if you do study yourself, you may discover you truly are not effective. There is irony in this dual role.

The type of teacher research Jennifer and I engaged in for this study is, at its heart, a process of self-scrutiny by the teacher. This particular process is a much bigger risk for the teacher than for the students. The students are considered to be the clients in this case. It is assumed with this approach to teacher research that if the teaching is not going well and students are not performing up to their potential, then something is wrong with the teaching—not with the students. This is a revolution in classroom research because the mirror is now placed in front of the teacher instead of in front of the students.

At greatest risk for me as a teacher researcher, I believe, was maintaining the integrity of the research process despite the previously mentioned risks to me as a teacher. Would I compromise the hard research questions that had to be asked in order to protect my integrity, my self-image, and my reputation as a teacher? I truly see a conflict of interest here. This is a potentially critical obstacle that could keep the truth about the classroom experience from ever emerging. This may be why improvements in student achievement in inner-city schools rarely take place: teachers simply aren't able to dig deep enough into the possible causes of this "low achievement." Finding that they are responsible might be too unbearable for teachers and too much of a sacrifice for them to make, even when such a sacrifice could very possibly benefit their students in the long run.

AS A POSSIBLE RACIST

The risk of discovering that I was a racist did not occur to me. I knew that my view about the causes of African American students' "low achievement" had changed in graduate school. Unlike my earlier opinion that these students were inferior to White, middle-class students, my belief now was that they were just as capable of success as any other students in school but were being evaluated based on very limited criteria. I saw these students as oppressed by a system set up by and for White, middle-class Americans and their children.

Although the issue of racial and cultural differences had come up in recent years in conversations with other educators and I had considered those differences as potential issues between my students and myself, I still was not convinced. Even though I realized that I myself was the product of the very system of which I was now critical, at the outset of my work with Jennifer, I did not see myself as a racist or that racial and cultural differences could undermine my goals as a teacher of African American students. It wasn't until I was deeply immersed in our work that I became aware of a racist attitude (inadvertently leading to racist behavior) underneath that recently awakened side of me. It was then that the possibility of my being a racist occurred to me and loomed as a risk of this work for me.

As the study progressed, I began to worry about this idea of myself as a racist. My students were very different from me, and it was hard not to judge them critically, since my own attitudes and behavior as a student had always been encouraged and validated. Such attitudes and behavior were "the norm" as far as my worldview was concerned, so that the differences I experienced with my inner-city students struck me initially as "abnormal" or "bad" rather than merely different. My expectations and notions about classroom life were molded by my child-hood experiences in school. I was a product of a White, middle-class upbringing, and as I have explained in an earlier chapter, this did not include any contact at all with African Americans.

The risk was that even though I thought I believed in the academic potential of these students and wanted them to succeed, I would not be able to understand their attitudes and behavior and be able to support and encourage them to the point where I could be an effective teacher for them.

AS A COLLEAGUE OF FELLOW TEACHERS

I must admit that, in the beginning, I did not consider our work together to be a threat to my relationship with fellow teachers. I became aware of this risk when I experienced skepticism from some faculty members in response to a presentation we gave during a faculty meeting. I realized that disclosing my own racist attitudes and behaviors as a White teacher could be threatening to the other teachers' self-images as White teachers. I became worried that in order to protect themselves, some of them might reject our research completely and distance themselves from us. The implications of our findings might cause the entire study to be criticized and ignored. As the research progressed, I anticipated an increasingly aloof attitude toward me, perhaps even alienation, from my colleagues, which might include polite but not friendly interactions.

As it turns out, I do not believe that my relationship with the faculty has been damaged by this work. However, for the most part, there has been very little interest expressed by the White teachers and administrators, and some have reacted in a defensive way to my story.

AS A COLLABORATOR

There were many rewards that came from my collaboration with Jennifer, but there were also concerns that emerged over time about the potential direction that our professional relationship could take. Jennifer and I embarked on our classroom study as near strangers, and because of the kids, we opened up to each other and shared our beliefs about the students and our views on many aspects of the classroom experience. There were several sensitive issues that we both grappled with, making us vulnerable to criticism from each other. We documented our experiences, using the research methods that are described in the appendix, and accumulated a great deal of rich data. As the first year of our study unfolded, we both began to realize the importance of the work we were doing, and that view was reinforced as we began to present our study at conferences and to write a journal article about it. As Jennifer completed her dissertation about our work and was considering getting it published on her own, I recognized a risk that comes with collaboration that I had not anticipated. I was worried that if she published our work on her own, I would not get any credit for it. Jennifer describes this risk for her as a new academic in her risk section below. I was not interested at the time in an academic career, but I was very invested in our work, as we have described.

Because I was looking at publication of the data in this light, Jennifer and I did face a critical period when she told me she was talking to publishers about a book by herself based on her dissertation. The prospect of Jennifer publishing what I perceived as our work on her own before I did, upset me very much. However, after consulting with several professors at UC Berkeley, I realized that Jennifer's dissertation (and any book based on it) was indeed her property and that I could write and publish my own version of the study. But I must admit that although I accepted Jennifer's position after talking to the professors, I was disappointed that our first major publication (whether written by her or by me) would not be a collaborative one.

This experience for both of us was a turning point in our relationship that laid bare our lack of trust in each other. Fortunately, we were ultimately able and willing to face and resolve our differences.

AS A PERSON

The biggest risk by far for me was the possibility of disillusionment with myself as a teacher, as a researcher, and as a human being. Once I was working with Jennifer in my classroom, I became aware of the obstacles that I faced as a White teacher wanting to be the best teacher possible for my students. But would I be able to overcome those obstacles? Did I have the courage, resolve, strength, and confidence to persevere as Jennifer guided me through this journey of discovery and change? I couldn't even imagine the pain, self-doubt, and insecurities that I would experience—often as my own worst critic.

I was afraid of what I might find out about myself and even more afraid of how I would cope with that truth. Could I survive such close scrutiny? Could I learn from my mistakes and improve as a teacher in an urban school, or would I retreat to the suburbs? Would I "get" what Jennifer was trying to tell me about my students and about me as their teacher? Or would I give up? I was putting myself out on a very shaky limb that could break at any time from the pressures of the study both on me and on Jennifer. How would our relationship evolve given what transpired in the classroom and what we learned about me? Would this journey strengthen our respect for each other and our resolve to pursue this work or would it destroy both?

JENNIFER'S RISKS

Initially I did not see any risks for myself in this collaboration. I was not invested in Karen's success or failure. This study was a curiosity project, a "look and see" at what White teachers were like as teachers of African American students. I confess now that I really did not trust Karen at that time. I used to refer to her as "the White woman I'm working with." She was nameless and faceless in my life outside of a collaboration about which I still held a lot of doubt; I wasn't convinced that our work together would make a difference in the students' lives. I saw it as making no real difference in my life as a teacher. I already knew that I was an effective teacher of African American children in ways that Karen was not. Although her students were responding positively to Karen's alternative teaching strategies and grading system, she was having behavioral problems with the students that were adversely affecting her efforts, and she had said as much to me. That was why I was in her class. And if it turned out that she could not become a more effective teacher with African American students, that would be her problem, not mine or the students'. These students were accustomed to having teachers, many of them White, who did not meet their needs, so they could cope with an unsuccessful experiment if that was what our collaboration turned out to be.

However, the more invested I became in Karen's success—especially after surviving our first tumultuous interactions surrounding the questionnaire (as discussed in an earlier chapter)—the more evident the risks became. These risks stem primarily from the fact that my lived experience in this country has taught me to be wary of relationships with White people. Such a commitment is dangerous to the well-being of my Black personhood, because there's a sense that an inevitable bad turn in the relationship will come: The question isn't how but when.

TRUSTING A WHITE PERSON

A connecting thread permeates my notions of risks in the collaboration between Karen and me. This thread is a lifelong nurturing of self-protection as an African American person against the potential threat embodied in every White person in America. Distrust of White people is nurtured in every African American child as part of his or her ethos of existence in America. I believe that perhaps this is similar to the way a lingering sense of African American inferiority continues to exist in the minds of White and other American people (including African Americans). And the two are most definitely linked. As an African American person you ask yourself, "How can I trust someone who thinks, consciously or subconsciously, that something is wrong with me to the extent that this *something* (tangible only in terms of physical difference) makes me an inferior human being?"

Baldwin (reprinted 1996) observed similar contradictions in his "talk to teachers" more than 50 years ago. He stated that on the one hand, an African American child is born into a country whose flag guarantees liberty and justice for all, but, on the other hand,

> this child is also assured by his countrymen that he is not, nor will he ever be, valued as a full citizen of his country, because he has never contributed

anything to civilization—that his past is nothing more than a record of humiliations gladly endured . . . and that the value he has as a Black man is proven by one thing only—his devotion to White people. If you think I am exaggerating, examine the myths which proliferate in this country about Negroes. (p. 220)

In describing his own identity struggle, Baldwin tells teachers that

in order for me to live, I decided very early that . . . I was not a "nigger" even though you [White America] called me one. But if I was a "nigger" in your eyes, there was something about you—there was something you needed. I had to realize when I was very young that I was none of those things I was told I was. So where we are now is that a whole country of people believe that I'm a "nigger," and I *don't*, and the battle's on! Because if I'm not what I've been told I am, then it means that you're not what you thought you were *either*! And that is the crisis. (pp. 223–224)

The sentiments expressed by Baldwin are symbolic of the foundation on which the African American's distrust of White Americans is based.

Let me qualify the distrust to which I refer, for there are several kinds, and to discuss all are beyond the scope of this chapter. The distrust to which I refer is not, in many cases, linked to hatred or fear. Rather, this distrust is equivalent to a parent's concern for his or her child who develops a penchant for playing with fire but who may be unaware of the potential danger involved in such play. In the African American lived experience, awareness of the danger is paramount because reliance on the power structures in society is necessary. And these structures are dominated by White people to such an extent that Black people are forced to play with fire in many instances (e.g., employment, housing, schooling, etc.).

Continuing with the fire metaphor, one may choose to play with the fire (as opposed to resisting it); that is, seek friendships with White people and ignore the societal imbalance of power that influence even individual friendships. For a while it seems that an equal relationship of mutual respect is unfolding. However, extenuating circumstances such as a high wind may cause the fire inadvertently to burn us; or a sudden rain may cause the fire's support and nourishment to die. "High wind" and "sudden rain" aptly describe how fickle the incidents and misunderstandings sometimes are that change relationships between White and African American people in America, and the disillusionment that usually follows widens the gap that already exists between the races. Stereotypes and legacies of distrust are often reaffirmed.

It is easy for one person to say to another, "Forgive me" in two situations: The first is when the person asking for forgiveness has no idea about the rawness of the emotional nerve that was struck in the other person. The second is when the person feels justified asking for forgiveness because he or she "didn't mean it." They never intended to cause hurt. It is important to highlight the anger that results from the hurt felt by Black people in both instances.

Whether or not pain is intentionally or unintentionally inflicted, it is still felt, and the person who inflicts the pain is responsible to some degree for the outcome. However, what gets complicated in this analysis is conveying that the anger felt by African Americans in these circumstances, similar to my earlier statements about distrust, is not the same as anger based on hate or fear. This anger, after it has run its course, does take into account that the pain was unintentionally inflicted, and therein lies the potential for understanding and forgiveness.

This pattern of interaction—of feeling unintended pain, then hurt and anger; getting over the anger, finding it in yourself to forgive, and remaining ever conscious that such mistakes can occur again and again—takes its toll. My involvement with Karen did at times follow such a pattern. Thus, a large part of the risk in our collaboration was the process of establishing trust.

To be able to teach Karen, I had to trust that she could learn. This type of trust is what I demand of all teachers of African American students: To be able to teach African American children, a teacher has to trust that they can learn. In my collaboration with Karen I had to practice what I preached. Learning to trust her is an ongoing lesson and an ongoing risk, and it is complicated by the dynamics between African Americans and White Americans that I've just described. In this case, although Karen's Whiteness is a symbolic barrier for which she cannot be held responsible, her understanding of how her Whiteness could act as such a barrier has been helpful to my process of sorting out the real versus imagined aspects of this barrier.

BEING A SELLOUT TO THE AFRICAN AMERICAN COMMUNITY

Another result of African Americans' distrust of White Americans is a distrust of African Americans who are perceived to be "close" to White Americans. Other African Americans often feel that such people give up a piece of their Blackness to be able to accomplish such a feat. And they do. In my case it was a part of my Black ethos that nurtured the self-protecting, automatic distrust of anyone who was White. I don't know if I can ever entirely give up this part of my ethos. However, rather than rid myself of it totally, I now check for any distortions that may result, and I am less quick to assign every event as occurring "because I am Black."

But this is much easier said than done, and in the midst of this, other African Americans may hold someone like me suspect. After 2 or so years of my working with Karen and presenting at a number of conferences, it was conveyed to me that some African American scholars were skeptical about my work with Karen. Somehow, these statements did not bother me. However, they introduced the possibility of my being perceived as a "sellout." Elsewhere (Obidah, in press) I detail the work of Mitchell (1996), who discusses this dilemma. Mitchell explains that "selling out" "connotes a permanence, a closure, and a denial of culture" (p. 83), and she sees this choice as "the ultimate compromise that a Black researcher can make" (p. 83). She notes that as social scientists, African Americans "are continually at risk, vulnerable to charges from either side of having sold out or of being written off as nothing more than an agitator rather than a serious academic" (p. 83). This potential to be perceived as a sellout was a significant professional risk in the collaboration between Karen and me.

With regard to this particular risk however, the African American students in Karen's class served as a helpful marker. I utilized students' responses to me as indicators of whether I was "keeping it real" for them. These students were not shy in their responses to either Karen or me, and it was important to both of us for students to give their input, whether or not we were ready to hear what the students wanted to say. I let the students' responses—in both formal and informal interactions—inform me of where I stood in terms of their perception of me as a sellout. I received no such indicators from them.

DEVELOPING AS A SCHOLAR

Karen, with important feedback from a colleague and friend, Mary-Lynn Lidstone, wrote the proposal that eventually led to our first presentation at the American Educational Research Association (AERA), in 1994. I was excited to be able to go to New Orleans and present at an educational conference. I would learn only later during my job search how important appearances at AERA are viewed as markers of one's potential to succeed in academe.

Still, attending AERA began my contemplation about the possibility of entering the academic profession, and the risks of our work pertaining to such a decision followed not long after. First and foremost, Karen and I were improving the teacher-student relationship in her classroom with the goal of improving the academic achievement of her African American students. Second, but more important in the academic context, we were conducting "a study," and part of conducting a study includes publications and recognition for one's contributions to the educational research literature.

Karen and I had talked about entering academe, and she initially felt that this was not where she wanted her career to go. She wanted to continue to do research from the vantage point of a classroom teacher. I, however, once I made the decision to enter this profession, strategized every action in terms of making myself marketable. Karen encouraged me to make our study the basis of my dissertation, and she was helpful as I developed my ideas regarding the perspective of the study that my dissertation would represent. I continued to work in Karen's classroom during the following year while I wrote my dissertation.

Another proposal we wrote based on the study was accepted for presentation at the 1995 AERA conference in San Francisco. We had not discussed—and I did not think it was necessary to—how aggressive I would be in terms of getting my dissertation published. I know now that Karen saw the writing of my dissertation and the publishing of a book based on it as two different activities. She saw the dissertation as fulfilling a requirement for school. The publication of a book based on the data was a matter that we would discuss when the time came.

Since these thoughts were not raised between us at the time, I did not know about Karen's perspective. I saw the dissertation and its publication as one and the same. I was being encouraged by my professors to publish my dissertation as a natural aspect of making myself marketable for the profession. At the 1995 AERA conference, I gave chapters of my dissertation to editors who I thought might be interested in publishing it. Karen felt disillusioned by my actions and her hurt led to her being a threat to the publication of my dissertation.

She asked if we could get together for coffee on the last day of the conference. We met at Starbucks, and Karen said that she had talked to a friend about the possibility that my dissertation would be published. Her friend had expressed concern that if I preempted Karen in publishing our work alone, that—given her impression of academe—I would get all of the credit and recognition for our work. Any subsequent publishing from Karen would be anticlimactic. Karen then told me that she felt that I should agree to have her as coauthor of my dissertation if it were accepted for publication. In the instant I heard Karen's statements, my mental image of her shifted from friend to enemy; from "Karen" to "White person." In my mind I thought, "Here is why it is not safe to work with, nor trust, White people. How could this woman feel that my dissertation was our work? I know that this is definitely the end of this collaboration." Insult was added to injury because she had let the advice of someone else—another White person—ruin what might have been a real friendship between two people of different racial and cultural backgrounds.

I told Karen no, that I would not make her coauthor. To my surprise, she asked, "Why not?" Outwardly calm, I explained that both of us had the same data set, but that my coding and analysis (at the time I said, "my story") of that data belonged to me. The product was MY STORY. I told her that she had her own story to write, which she should begin as soon as possible. Then she said, in effect, that if I pursued the publication of my dissertation without her as coauthor, she would call the publisher and say that my work was not valid. Outraged inside yet outwardly composed, I told her to do whatever she felt she had to do and I would do the same. I then said that I thought the conversation was finished, and I stood up to leave. Believe it or not, we hugged. I went home and called my advisor, and amid tears and admonitions about trusting White people, from both her and myself, we strategized the legal battle we were prepared to fight. I didn't expect Karen to change her mind, and knowing that I was right, I was prepared to wage the war she had started.

However, a few days later, yellow daisies arrived with a note of apology from Karen and a request to meet. I got angry all over again, because now I had to be "civil" and forgive—since she was willing to admit she was wrong. But, I asked myself, at what cost was this forgiveness? The cost was leaving myself open, yet again, to another cycle of pain, anger, temporary peace (there is a temporary measure of peace in severing friendships with such potential to harm), and then forgiveness.

I should say that today, after many hours of reflective dialogue, I understand that Karen felt disappointed and betrayed. She later told me that she had thought that after she explained her feelings about publishing a single-author book based on the data, I would agree with her. At that time, however, I saw her actions as justification of that distrust I mentioned earlier that African Americans have of White Americans. I perceived her actions, particularly the last statement of the conversation, as an attempt to sabotage my career.

As I reflected on that day over the years, I came to believe that if Karen had come to me and voiced her worries and fears in a less threatening manner, we would have reached some agreement with which we both could have lived. However, our communication started off on the wrong foot. She had consulted someone about me without talking to me first, and then she had presented me with the conclusion of their conversation as a directive that I should follow (that is, making her a coauthor). When I didn't agree, Karen became threatening and I reacted, all of which led to further miscommunication. This spiral of miscommunication is an example of the fickle nature of what can go wrong in a cross-race relationship.

Neither of us knows how our relationship would have turned out if Karen had not solicited advice from several of her professors who agreed with my position. But I confess that it took a long time to rebuild the fledgling trust that had started to grow between us. For me, the hardest part of all this was realizing that I *had* to take action to continue our work together. I could not allow my feelings of anger to fester, and yet those feelings lingered for some time, despite my best efforts. Our work was important for the kids, for the many African American students Karen would teach in the future.

My Buddhist prayers about the situation coupled with memories of our past 2 years of success fueled my desire to continue to work with Karen. The importance of a White teacher's improved teaching and rapport with African American students that had the potential to positively affect these students' academic achievement could not be disregarded. White teachers constitute the majority of teachers working with African American students in schools, and few were as willing as Karen to reflect on and improve their practice to better serve these students. Our success in her classroom could not be taken lightly. For me, success was observing the positive results of my guidance and interventions and feeling the satisfaction of putting the well-being of African American students first over any reservations I had about working with a White woman. These successes supported our reconciliation.

In the process of rebuilding the trust between us, Karen and I went to South Africa and presented our work together, and we continued to talk about what had occurred. We returned to the United States, and even though I moved from northern California soon after our return to the United States, Karen invited me to continue to work with her. For one additional year I analyzed notes from her classroom for emerging patterns and offered her guidance on how to progress and improve relationships with her African American students. Her invitation that I continue working with her also helped to rebuild our relationship, because this action indicated to me that she cared more about making her classroom better for African American students than she cared about any potential threats I posed regarding the publication of the work.

After a while, we stopped discussing the incident that had occurred in Starbucks, and not until we began to write this book was it revisited. In the intervening 2 years we became friends. I got married and Karen was there. Karen's children graduated from college, one daughter got married, and I shared her joy. Karen was diagnosed with breast cancer, and we rallied through her illness together. We spent time at each other's homes and with each other's families over the years. Sitting at my kitchen table in the spring of 1997, reading through the data, it occurred to me to call Karen and ask her to write this book with me. I saw that Karen was an integral part of the story, and at that time, since we had become close friends, I felt that we could write the book together. I still believed that we each had our own individual story to tell. The way that this book is structured embodies the many ways that our respective processes—our thoughts, our actions, our emotions, what mattered to us at different moments—were different. At the time I called, however, it just felt right that we should tell our stories together.

ANTICIPATING THE DIFFICULTIES

Through the story of our study, we want to convey to the reader just how difficult it is for researchers who are racially and culturally different, as Karen and I are, to work together, especially when "race" is at the heart of the study. This process is not easy and may test the core of one's values and belief systems.

This type of research is fairly unique, we believe, and we plunged into it without any preconceived notions of what the process might be. We were making our own way, often feeling blind and rudderless. The risk factors we have described here loomed over us and were a constant reminder of our vulnerability and of the potential pitfalls inherent in the kind of research we were attempting. We hope that by writing about the risks, both anticipated and unexpected, that we took as part of doing this study—by sharing our experiences—we can save those who undertake such a collaboration from some of the miscommunication and pain we endured.

CHAPTER 6

On Cultural Conflict in the Classroom: Lisa Delpit Dialogues with the Authors

WHEN WE CONCEIVED of this book, both of us were aware of Lisa Delpit's work pertaining to the sociocultural contexts of African American students' academic achievement. Delpit's (1988) early conceptions of how "the culture of power" [her term] influences interactions between teachers and students helped us to understand elements of the dynamics that took place between Karen and her students during the first year of the study. In light of the usefulness of her work in furthering our understanding of how to teach African American students effectively, we sent Lisa early drafts of chapters of this book along with a request for a conversation with her. She agreed to talk to us about our work, and this chapter is the result of our dialogue.

The interview took place in Georgia on December 15, 1998, and lasted for 3 hours. This conversation condenses 170 pages of transcription and has been edited for clarity. Additionally, the themes that evolved from our conversation were formatted to parallel the order of similar themes discussed in the previous chapters. These themes are reflected in the headings throughout the conversation.

We invite you to "listen in."

REFLECTIONS ON "HERSTORIES"

LISA: I was interested in the fact that both of you mentioned television as playing important roles in your early histories [see chapter 1].

You didn't go into detail, but I feel it is such a powerful force, for you Jennifer, in particular sitting in Barbados watching American television. What about the White people on TV? Were they all that you saw?

JENNIFER: Yes, the White people on TV were what I thought of as the accurate representations of life in America. White people were the norm. On the island there were always two sides to life, a White side and a Black side. I remember even as a child, if we had White guests—my father was a taxi driver, and he used to bring a lot of tourists to our home—we had to speak properly, but it was for their sake. Speaking Standard English to the White tourists didn't mean that the language we normally spoke was wrong. We spoke Standard English to *help them* understand us. It was as if we were versed in their language and our own language, and in the interest of hospitality we spoke to them in their language. Definitely there was a way to be around White people in terms of language, but there was also a way to be around your own people, and the two weren't thought of as connecting.

LISA: Karen, you mentioned watching *Leave It to Beaver* and *Ozzie and Harriet*. I wondered how you saw those shows relating to your life? Particularly early on.

KAREN: Very similar. My mom was at home, and did a lot of volunteering. We'd get home from school, and there'd be snacks in the kitchen. She was at our beck and call basically.

And my mom and dad didn't fight, so it was all very idyllic—just like it was portrayed in those TV shows. My mom seemed happy all during my childhood although I later found out that she didn't feel completely fulfilled because as a woman in the fifties she wasn't able to pursue her professional interests in life. But while we were growing up, we never would have known that by the way she acted.

JENNIFER: How do you mean your parents didn't fight?

KAREN: They hardly ever argued.

LISA: At least not that you saw.

KAREN: Not that I saw. There were times when my mother got mad at my father for things and might not speak to him for a day or so, but it wouldn't go on and on, and there wouldn't be screaming and yelling. That was very, very rare. I've talked to my brothers about that too, about how we developed a notion about relationships—that they're always harmonious; there aren't any problems, and you don't argue with each other. Generally we were in a working-class neighborhood, mostly blue collar, and mothers stayed at home. The kids would come home from school and play outside, and you never saw police. You never knew that there could be any problems in the city, or drug-related problems. Fear of harm was something that was completely nonexistent in those shows too, I think. I mean there were never any problems other than little family things that would come up—personality conflicts or differences in values or perceptions—but it all could be talked out. Like in *Father Knows Best*, the father comes in, sits down with you, and helps you work it all through. I don't remember much tension.

JENNIFER: I think that's something we have in common, Karen and I. I didn't grow up in Barbados with any fear either, and White people were a novelty in my life—tourists. They came, we smiled at them, and then they left. We had a couple of pen pals, stuff like that, but no fear around them at all. Growing up in my neighborhood, the presence of White people wasn't an everyday thing.

LISA: Life in your neighborhood sounds like it was a cocoon.

JENNIFER: Yes.

LISA: That's how I felt in many ways in my neighborhood as well, but we always had to deal with the outside, and whenever it was dealing with the outside, that's when the problems with White people came up. Let me ask you this: Was your household like Karen's? Was there no arguing and everybody got along?

JENNIFER: No.

LISA: Was there a lot of loud arguing?

JENNIFER: There was loud arguing. We had arguments. We were exposed to all of the grown-up problems. But there was a built-in feeling that I had as a child. The adults let me see what was going on, but they also made it clear that these things did not affect their love and care for me. Their belief was that they were not going to pretend that everything was all right when it wasn't, but they conveyed to me that, regardless of the situation that was occurring at the moment, I was going to be all right. I was secure in the fact that my parents would always take care of me to the very best of their abilities.

PERCEPTIONS OF AFRICAN AMERICAN STUDENTS

LISA: I wonder if you hear the differences in your family interactions and how that might later affect communication styles with African American students and each other. I think this relates to Jennifer's relationship with the kids that you both talk about [see chapter 2], how Jennifer was the authoritarian in class and the so much more informal buddy out of class.

JENNIFER: I've always felt that I can't just deal with a student through the role of "student" because that wasn't the whole of them. Being a student was something they had to do to become educated. But if I, as their teacher, didn't find a way to find out everything else about them, neither of us could perform those roles well. I never separated the roles of student from the kids' roles of sister, aunt, cousin, brother, and so forth. I'm talking about finding a way to let the kids acknowledge that those other relationships play a part in their development as well. So that if . . . on the playground . . . they get in a fight with somebody in another class and they say, "Well, this person bothered my cousin yesterday," I'm not gonna say, "Well this person didn't bother you, the student." It's important to them that they respond to the role of cousin, even in the context of school. They can't just pretend, "I'm a student, and I'm in Ms. Obidah's class, I am her student and that's all I am." They believe instead that, "I gotta be my cousin's cousin all the time, in school and everywhere I go. And that person bothered my cousin."

My interactions with them recognized that they were somebody's cousin. First I acknowledged that relationship, then I addressed the issue of fighting. In fact, they believed that by acknowledging the relationship with their cousin, which was the basis of the fight, I can then judge the event of fighting more fairly, because I had all the facts.

These types of interactions with my students occurred mostly outside of the class. For example, one of my students' moms was a bus driver, and her route passed in front of the school. Sometimes, she would stop the bus, and the student would tell me that she needed to go to her mom to get her lunch money. At that point I couldn't say, "You're in class, you can't go to your mom." The mom can't leave the bus because she's on her job. And it's none of my business why this transaction did not take place before the school day started. I just nodded, the child ran to the bus and got her lunch money, the mother waved to me, I waved back as she drove off, the student ran back to class, and school resumed. In these ways I acknowledged that their lives didn't stop just because they were in school.

KAREN: But how did you come to believe that? Was it experiences that you'd had earlier—when you were working with teenagers in some other capacity?

JENNIFER: To say how did you come to know that is to frame such knowledge like it was a realization. That's my life. That's how I was raised. You don't separate family from being a student.

I hear a lot of teachers talking about the notion that there's a time and a place for everything. But their time and their place—how they define it—may be different from mine and probably from the students' and their families' definition of time and space. You know what I mean? That idea of time and place affects my relationship with my students, because I often concede to their definitions.

LISA: All of this is espoused in an African notion of the integration of all parts of you that Asa Hilliard (1992) talks about. You are never one thing. You are always all of those pieces and connections. You cannot talk about affective versus cognitive nor about aesthetic versus academic because it is all one. I think that's a very strong feature that goes through a lot of African cultures and African descendants.

KAREN: Jennifer, you felt that you needed to respond to the whole child, not just in their role as a student, but to their life outside and everything. I think that I probably did that with my White students, but I didn't do it with African American kids.

LISA: So do you think you were more connected to the White kids than you were to the African American students?

KAREN: I do. I think that part of it was familiarity and the feeling that we had a lot in common, and that I could say and do whatever I wanted to. I didn't have any concerns about being a racist, about my actions being interpreted a certain way and being kind of worried about that interpretation affecting my relationship with the kids. And I was very strict because I felt like that's what their parents wanted, but because I thought that there were differences in the way my African American students thought and the way they'd been raised, I was not sure how to work with them.

LISA: What made you think that? Was it the way they responded to you? Or was it sort of an expectation before you went in?

KAREN: It was definitely an expectation before I got there, and it was mostly from things I'd read. It certainly wasn't a result of talking to African American adults or kids. I'd had some experience—when I first started teaching—with African American kids at the mostly White school where I taught. They came out in buses, and I was told that I needed to teach them in a very different way, be much more structured, and simplify the curriculum.

JENNIFER: You were told these things?

KAREN: I can't remember the actual conversations, but I know that I was designing curriculum for the inner-city kids with another teacher in the district. We agreed—we both came to the decision—that we needed to teach the kids in a different way. I'm trying to remember where I got that impression. I guess it was from the test scores. I think it probably was in meetings where administrators were saying, "Now these kids are coming from a different kind of situation, and their skills are really low based on their test scores. Their attention span is shorter."

JENNIFER: They got all of that from test scores?

KAREN: I think it was hearsay, I really do. They never had any experience with these kids, and they just assumed. I was expecting the kids to be very difficult and so I was ready for them. The principal said, "Throw them out if you have a problem, and then pretty soon they'll get the message, and they'll follow along with you. They'll fall in line."

Another thing I was thinking about was how you were saying, Jennifer, that you felt that you needed to respond to the whole child and be thinking about everything about the student. You wouldn't just think about their role as a student, but their life outside and everything. I think that I probably did that with my White kids, but I didn't do it with my African American students when I first started working with them and later during my dissertation research. My explanation for this is that I felt like an outsider. I felt like I would be an intruder. I would be invading their privacy by trying to get close to them, and I didn't think they wanted me to because of the cultural differences that I imagined. I thought that would make them uncomfortable and suspicious and standoffish.

JENNIFER: But did *you* want to?

KAREN: Yeah, I did. I felt that I had changed a lot. I really believed in these kids and I wanted the best for them, and I believed that they would sense that. I felt that they could tell because, previously, I'd been told by my White kids that they could tell that I really cared about them. I was trying new things to make it more interesting. So I thought that the energy in that caring would be obvious to my African American students and that they would respond positively to it.

When they didn't, then I had no idea what was going on. And other teachers said, "Oh, you have to try the Fred Jones method because it's very effective," where you offer rewards to the students and then you have a stopwatch that you use. If they're not listening, you turn that stopwatch on, and all that time is taken away from the reward at the end of the week. And you stand there and stare at them if they're talking. You don't say a word. You put your hands behind your back, and you just stand there and stare at them. I thought, "Okay, I'll try that." I thought I needed to use some techniques like that.

I didn't imagine that it was partly who *I* was that was causing the problem. I thought I was very objective and very professional and that I loved the kids and I wanted them to do well. But there was a limit to that, in terms of the relationship, because I was afraid. I really think I was afraid and nervous for the same reason that I was afraid and nervous about getting closer to you, Jennifer, by sharing myself, by opening up more.

CONFLICTING COMMUNICATION STYLES

KAREN: I also assumed that Jennifer thought differently than I, because she's African American. I assumed that the way she saw things, the way she responded, and what her feelings were would be different from mine. So I needed to talk to her in a different way. I mean I wasn't sure how to talk to her [see chapter 3]. So, I kind of had to rehearse . . . with my husband. I had to think through what I thought because if I wasn't sure what I thought or if I was not at all clear on what I wanted to say, I was reluctant and uncomfortable talking to her.

JENNIFER: But you see, those words "techniques" and "rehearse"— there's some fakeness to them for me. There's some detachment, objectivity. Those words are not synonymous with a *real* relationship.

LISA: To you.

JENNIFER: To me, they're not. Even with good intentions, it's still fake.

LISA: So it's reason and objectivity in one cultural stance versus involvement and emotion in the other cultural stance. Also, it is almost inevitable that you would have communication problems with someone from a very different background. When you discussed your families earlier, it seemed that whatever the problem was in your home, Karen, it was kept from the children. And in your case, Jennifer, it was, everybody get your point out now or you're not gonna get your point out at all [laughter]. And you expect, if somebody has something on their mind, they bring it up. And it's out there and you say it. And that was one of the things that I think caused you all some conflict, because you're expecting, if something's on Karen's mind, Karen's gonna say it.

JENNIFER: Just say it! [laughter]. Karen's expecting that since we have to build a relationship here the only way to keep it going is to keep everything on an even keel. If we start yelling, that's the end.

KAREN: That's the way I was teaching too. That's the way I was looking at the kids, that I wanted to maintain the relationship and make sure it was a good one and not disrupt it with conflict.

LISA: And a good one is one—?

KAREN: Is one with no conflict.

LISA: [turning to Jennifer] And a good relationship is?

JENNIFER: Bring it out! Let's talk about it, duke it out, work it out and then keep going.

LISA: I don't know if you ever saw the movie *Jerry McGuire*, but my favorite line is from the character played by Cuba Gooding when he was arguing with Jerry. The argument was escalating, and Jerry says, "I can't communicate with you if you keep yelling and screaming." And Cuba Gooding says the equivalent of "See, the way I see it is we've just *started* communicating." That portrayal of the differences in communication styles between Black and White people is true.

JENNIFER: I think that's a deep and unique distinction. I mean a lot of times people say we don't have the words to talk about race. But we're talking about . . . I don't want to call it style.

LISA: It is cultural style, I think.

JENNIFER: I'll agree to attach "cultural" to "style," but what I'm referring to is not just an out-of-the-blue occurrence. It's . . .

LISA: Deeply embedded. And you view other people through it.

JENNIFER: Yes. Which is a notion that is deeper than style. Style, to me, implies something that is changeable. But we're talking about something that's embedded in the way you've grown up. So, you can't change it. You can't even articulate it for the most part because it's so much a part of you.

LISA: Black folk will often think that White people are being evasive and deceitful almost by not being what they [Black folk] consider as forthright and honest. Whereas White people think Black folk are about to just go off the deep end [laughter] I mean just blow up—blow up and maybe turn to violence. White people don't seem to be accustomed to this level of emotional expressiveness coming from someone who wants to continue a relationship. If they get to that point, they're expecting that it means the end of the relationship.

KAREN: And they don't know what to do with it either. They don't know how to handle it or respond to it, and that's probably why a lot of times it just ends. I mean . . . because it's too frightening, and nobody likes that feeling of uncertainty and frustration.

JENNIFER: Maybe that's why when we had the tension around the questionnaire [chapter 3], you felt more comfortable talking to close White friends about it.

KAREN: Absolutely.

LISA: Because she was angry—upset and angry—and she couldn't bring that to you because that would destroy the relationship that you all were trying to build.

JENNIFER: But her actions pissed me off to no end.

LISA: And I'm sure that was a shock to Karen.

JENNIFER: Explain that to me.

LISA: Because she's trying to keep your relationship intact by getting herself together—defusing her anger and frustration by talking to other people, so then she can come back and be civil and keep a good relationship with you. Since a good relationship to Karen means that there's no conflict, she had to work out the conflict somewhere else so that she would not bring it back to you, but you can speak for yourself, Karen.

KAREN: I think that's exactly what it was. The only thing I would add is that I was afraid to admit my fears to you, Jennifer, because of the relationship that we'd had up until then which had to do with graduate school. I was already finished with my degree, and I'd been teaching for years and years, even though I had admitted to you that I was concerned about not being a good teacher with these kids.

JENNIFER: I still can't understand why you should go and talk to somebody else. At the time I was thinking: "Just say what you're gonna say, but say it to me."

LISA: I assume that a part of our African American heritage—and this pertains to Africans in the diaspora as well—is that our notion of building relationships includes a very open description and expression of feelings. To not express your emotions is viewed as deceit, disrespecting the person with whom you're trying to build a relationship. If you go around talking to others about that person, and you won't even talk to them, then you don't respect them. Whereas, Karen's view was, "I respect you so much, I'm going to defuse this anger so that when I come back to you, we can maintain our relationship."

KAREN: And I don't want to hurt your feelings, by telling you what I really think about what's going on.

JENNIFER: And you had no clue that not telling me hurt my feelings.

KAREN AND LISA: Right.

JENNIFER: But what made me angry with what I perceived as Karen's fakeness was that she came to me as a White person and said, "There's something wrong in my classroom and I want to make it better." So I felt like, Okay, here's somebody saying "Let's do whatever needs to be done to fix the problem." I thought that she had given me an invitation to be real. Instead, she started faking it again. So I'm thinking to myself, "Are we going to make an appointment to start addressing the issue? Is this how it's gonna play out?" Her reactions made me question why she brought me in the classroom. Was she bringing me there to validate her efforts no matter how effective they were with the kids? Or was she there to get at the heart of the matter?

What was unusual in such a situation of miscommunications and misconceptions is that we had that point of connection. We had the kids, and the only time we understood each other was when either of us said, "I'm doing it because of the kids." From the time she framed anything, "I'm doing it because of the kids," I gave her the benefit of the doubt. If I said, "I'm doing it because of the kids," she said, "Okay." But trying to figure it out, in terms of who we were, didn't make any sense.

LISA: That's interesting you say that. I believe that we're gonna waste a whole bunch of time and energy and get everybody mad if we start talking about race apart from talking about the kids.

[All agree.]

KAREN: Now, I was surprised that Jennifer didn't respect me more because here I was done with my degree at Berkeley, so I kind of figured, well there would be some more stature that I suddenly had, compared to being a student. And then that I had been teaching for so many years, and my reputation in the district was very positive and strong. Somehow

I figured she would have known that. She would have talked to people, she would have heard and just would have understood.

JENNIFER: The reason why I think my respect for Karen wasn't there was because she wasn't doing a good job of discipline and, as a result, of teaching the kids. Karen wasn't earning any respect as an authority figure from the kids or me. That classroom wasn't one where you could rest on your laurels. So what if you graduated from Berkeley? So what if you had a reputation as a good teacher in the district?

In that classroom, for the time that you were there, you were ineffective. As such, there wasn't any basis for respect even though there's a larger context of society that gives you this respect based on your doctorate and years of teaching experience. I don't find that what one holds in society has any impact in urban classrooms, between the teachers and the students.

LISA: I've been very interested in this issue of authority within the African American community [see chapter 4]. I've observed that it is not given with roles. It really is not. It is given based on who you are, what you prove about who you are, and in whatever context you happen to be.

Authority is not a given. As for presenting the authoritarian persona during classroom time, if it's done successfully and students begin to respond positively to that teacher's authority, I've found kids to say, "Yeah, she don't take nothing from nobody. Yeah, she's a good teacher. Yeah, she can handle that class." I think the issue of authority is another interesting cultural difference that also deserves some exploration.

JENNIFER: In order to establish your teacher authority, Karen, you go into a teacher mode, right?

KAREN: Yep.

LISA: By teacher mode you mean keeping your distance, being detached, and focusing on content instead of relationships—the traditional way of being a teacher.

JENNIFER: Right. But I don't define the traditional way of being a teacher as necessarily being an effective teacher.

LISA: Jennifer, Karen's response to her African American kids doesn't sound very different from how you initially responded to the Emory students. In some way, you did the teacher role too.

JENNIFER: Not at first, but I soon realized that students misinterpreted my use of humor. They couldn't see my cultural cues that the African American kids recognized. The African American kids knew when I was joking, and they knew when I was serious. The White kids mixed it all up. So I realized that my cultural cues were off with them, and what I did was resort to the cues I knew they knew, which was being very structured, no humor, stating the rules, being very serious, only lecturing, and so forth. Now I'm gradually weaving in the kind of teaching that I like to do. I'm learning about how good a teacher I can be with them. But before I could do that, I had to utilize what they needed, what they expected.

KAREN: How did you know what that was?

JENNIFER: I started to think about what was familiar to them.

LISA: And how you knew what was familiar to them was because you had to learn to do it yourself in school.

JENNIFER: That's right.

LISA: That's why you knew. That's one of the reasons why people of color—no matter what ethnicity they are in America—learn at least two cultures: their home culture and the public culture.

[All agree.]

LISA: Whereas Karen only learned her own culture because the schools and everything else were based on her culture. I think we haven't acknowledged in our teacher education programs that people of color can be a resource because they know typically both of these cultures and that White student teachers need some way of getting into the ones that they don't know.

JENNIFER: Because you, Karen, went to the kids expecting them to know what you all were taught, that norm, and those kids—quote/ unquote—were bad. They responded with "Give me something better than that 'cause that's not gonna work," and you, Karen, couldn't switch because you didn't know what to switch to.

LISA AND KAREN: Right.

LISA: And when you don't know, what do you do? What did you say you do when you don't know? You retreat to the familiar.

KAREN: But everyone wants something familiar so that they know how to act and know where others are coming from.

LISA: That's what we all do. We retreat to the familiar.

JENNIFER: It seems, though, that most teachers don't want the kids to go to the familiar in the classroom. That's what the kids are fighting right now. It's acknowledged that all human beings go to the familiar when they're uncomfortable, but when the kids go to what they're familiar with, such as using their home language, for example, teachers start to project all kinds of negative images onto what the kids are familiar with in their communities. Teachers think, "Who would want to go there?" and they want to keep all of that out of their classrooms.

LISA: Right. I think you're right. The teacher thinks of the African American students, "I can't let you go there." And like you mentioned, Jennifer, the system and schools tend to only see the kids' problems.

KAREN: All they hear about is the police being around, the crime and drugs and all the negatives. That's the only thing that you ever hear about.

JENNIFER: I don't even know that there's a way that others who do not live in similar conditions could understand life—that it's not all bad. Teachers have to understand a student's home life in ways other than in a negative light, to have a relationship with them.

LISA: Karen, you started doing a lot of different things, as Jennifer just said, after she left. But you made a statement that you don't think you could have changed your relationship with the kids or with, I assume, the people you're working with now, had you not forged a relationship with Jennifer. I was wondering if you could talk more about that?

KAREN: That struck me when I was rereading some of the data. I was asking myself why I changed the way I thought about the kids. I'm different now. I talk to them a lot more; I ask them questions; and I'm much more tuned into their lives. When they come in and they sit down or they're out in the halls, or whatever, I'm very anxious to learn more. And I know how important it is, and I know and feel that I can. I don't think that would have happened if Jennifer and I hadn't broken through certain barriers, certain ways that we were both resisting getting to know each other better.

So when you learn that about somebody who is from what you thought was a foreign culture, such a completely different group, then you start thinking very differently about every person who comes from that culture. And then you start wanting to have relationships with more and more of those people, whereas I was very nervous about that in the past. I was afraid.

I thought that African Americans would not want to know me because I'm White and because of the whole history of race relations in this country. I felt like they had a lot of anger toward White people and that it was going to interfere with a relationship. And I felt a certain amount of guilt and a certain amount of responsibility and concern about that. I don't even know that I would have acknowledged all of this without our relationship.

LISA: I sense from both of you a lot of emotion. Some of that needs to come out.

JENNIFER: One of the things I wanted us to talk about was the difficulties of being a mentor. People ask me what challenges there were for me in this work. Some of them seem to think that Karen was the only one affected by it. They think—because I took the assertive role, pushed the plate if you will, made Karen think about things—that I wasn't affected by having to do that over and over again.

I got tired of wondering why Karen couldn't just acknowledge certain things. Why couldn't she just be herself? Why couldn't we relate to each other as human beings? Why does there have to be a prescription for working with African American kids? Why does Karen have to be taught how to relate to African Americans? I didn't have to be taught how to relate to White people. Why do African Americans have to keep teaching White people how to relate?

KAREN: Now, I don't agree with that. I think African Americans learn how to relate to White people by being taught. How did you learn? You didn't just do it instinctively or from watching TV or from . . .

JENNIFER: But it's a different kind of teaching. It wasn't that I had to be given a lesson as an adult. It was already a part of my psyche. Why didn't it have to be a part of your psyche that you had to learn how to relate to Black people? For our own survival in this country, we have to learn there's a world here and there's a world there, but you White people could grow up and don't have to worry that another world exists outside your world. For us, we had to learn about your world; a world that for us could be potentially harmful if we weren't prepared for it.

LISA: You're expressing an anger at what Karen didn't have to learn. It's a kind of structural anger; it's not an anger directed at Karen, but an anger directed at the way society is structured. However, certain reactions from Karen resonated the unfairness and inequality embedded in the system. In this way, Karen's actions became symbolic of all that was wrong with the system. And you, Jennifer, become angry when you come face to face with these structural conditions through these symbolic interactions with Karen. But it's important for us to note that the anger is not directed at Karen personally. Interactions with another White person that resonated these structural conditions would produce the same feelings of anger in Jennifer, right Jennifer?

JENNIFER: Right. That's exactly right. On top of that, I held that anger in check because it wasn't an issue that I had with Karen the individual. I could've put my whole anger on her—which I didn't—but that didn't mean I didn't feel it, you know what I mean? And my frustration would sometimes anger me to the point where I felt like saying to Karen, "If you don't know it, I don't care. It's your business to know, not mine."

LISA: I understand that frustration, and I think it's important because people often view it as if they're doing us a favor to listen to us. It's as if they're saying to us, "You shouldn't feel pain or anger because here I am trying to be good by listening to you. So, why are you getting mad at me?"

JENNIFER: Right! [Laughter] They're saying, "I'm willing to admit my ignorance. This is your opportunity to teach me! So why are you upset? If I don't listen to you, you get upset. If I listen to you, you get upset. What am I supposed to do?"

LISA: Right, and it's very rational. It makes sense. But I think it's important to bring up that this is hard for you too. Yes, it's hard for Karen, but it's hard for you too.

KAREN: This is the first time that you've done anything like this?

JENNIFER: Yes. I had to stay with the process because we were invested in making that classroom better and until that classroom was better, I couldn't walk away. I was tired though! I was really tired sometimes, but I couldn't walk away. I learned about fatigue [laughter].

LISA: Were you surprised at how much anger you felt as you went through the process of working with Karen?

JENNIFER: I wasn't surprised at how much anger I felt. I was surprised at how much commitment I felt, how much investment I started to have in her being successful. And that brought on another set of anger . . . [laughter] . . . not the anger that I anticipated.

LISA: Which was?

JENNIFER: Anger about the racist things that would come out of her mouth. Knowing she was probably going to say something unintentionally racist and that I was going to be pissed off at her. For most White people I know, the world revolves around them, and they only see the world from where they are. So that anger I wasn't surprised at. I knew we were going to have those moments, but I didn't anticipate anger at knowing that I had to come back even when I didn't want to. At times I wished that there was a point where we both would have said, "Forget it." But there was always a point when if one of us said, "Forget it," the other one said, "Come on back." Then there was my wanting to trust her but she would do something to mess up that trust. Then I would have to build my desire up to want to trust her again and I'm doing all of this while *not knowing if I liked her or not!* [laughter].

KAREN: But didn't you think it was going to be hard when we started out?

JENNIFER: No, because I gave myself an out. I went in thinking, if it didn't work, so what? You're not going to be the first ineffective White teacher the kids would have had, and I can go on and do the work that I know I'm good at. I didn't anticipate being invested in you being a better teacher.

KAREN: And why do you think that happened?

JENNIFER: Because you were really trying, and changes were happening. If changes were not occurring in your classroom, maybe I would have bailed out. To come back to your class after the first year of our study, and to see the changes in your classes and in your attitude with the students was really encouraging. Those things made me say "Hey, maybe she did learn something! Maybe that struggle and pain were worth it."

FINAL REFLECTIONS

KAREN: Lisa, with the work that you've done, we'd love to know how this all fits into your way of thinking about these issues.

LISA: Well, I think it is so extraordinarily valuable. A lot of our White teachers and university professors have never been in a position where they had to learn about themselves from somebody else who was very different from them, or learn that there were other ways of interacting, or that there was systematic rule-governed behavior in other cultures that wasn't just "wrong" from their perspective.

When I heard of what you all were doing, I was very excited about it, and after reading what you've written, I'm even more excited about it. Your work together opens a door for people to realize that this is something that they could do, that this work is worthwhile doing, and that more educators need to do it.

KAREN: One of the things I'm hoping is that more teachers will really think about what their role is in all of this . . . that they're major players and that they may be contributing to what's going on.

LISA: Well, they are—for better or worse.

KAREN: They certainly are, but they don't think they are. An awful lot of teachers just won't go there at all. It's really hard to look at yourself critically and think that what you're doing may be causing this kind of behavior . . . kids not learning that well or whatever it is.

LISA: Right. I've done work with teacher research, and I realized that you can't do it by yourself, or you can't do it just with people who have the same perspectives as you do because you'll never get at what you don't know. That's the part that you need to get at.

KAREN: But I really do wonder, based on my own experience, whether it's possible to ever really understand and be effective unless a White teacher goes through something like this. You can take classes, and you can do a lot of reading, but I'd been in classes and I'd done a lot of reading, and it didn't make any difference. It changed my attitude towards the kids, but it didn't help me to understand the culture better or really see myself—what I say and what I am doing that is interfering with my effectiveness as a teacher. How can a teacher know that unless somebody else is observing them who's sensitive to those differences and who points them out. I can't imagine another way. And for teachers in the same school to help each other in this way would require a major overhaul of how we schedule classes and schedule time and so on in schools, but I really wonder whether there's any other way to do it.

LISA: I don't really think there is.

CHAPTER 7

For Those Who Dare: Toward Transforming Teaching Practices

WE OPEN this chapter with letters each of us wrote to explain why we think this work was so important. In our own way, each of us asks teachers of African American students to initiate a similar kind of self-reflective process with another person whose familiarity with and support of African American children has been successfully demonstrated. Of course, there are teachers who are not African American who are successful with African American students. However, we believe that teachers who are unfamiliar with African American students would be far more challenged and would learn more from engaging in such a process with a respected partner from the same background as their students.

At the same time, we are asking the African American community (both inside and outside of schools) to be open to this kind of collaborative partnership with teachers. Clearly, the process we advocate must include willing teachers and members of the African American community who have a deep understanding of and commitment to the academic success of African American children.

Following these letters is a set of recommendations and a final summary based on our work together. Additionally, we offer suggestions for those of you who may be interested in taking part in a project such as the one we've described.

TO ALL TEACHERS OF AFRICAN AMERICAN STUDENTS AND THEIR POTENTIAL MENTORS

KAREN'S LETTER

Those of us who work with inner-city African American students face an extremely difficult situation. Often our socioeconomic circumstances and cultural backgrounds put us worlds far apart from our students. Yet in order to serve them effectively, we need to understand our students and to nurture them so that they can achieve their potential. As you all know, African American students living in the inner cities of the United States have not been achieving on the same levels as middle-class, White students. Ladson-Billings (1996) writes:

> Ultimately, the work of education in a democracy is to provide opportunities for all citizens to participate fully in the formation of the nation and its ideals. These ideals can never be fully realized if significant portions of our society are excluded from high quality education and the opportunity to play public roles in society. African American students are suffering in our schools at an alarming rate. They continue to experience high drop out, suspension, and expulsion rates. While possessing a high school diploma is no guarantee of success in U.S. society, not having one spells certain economic and social failure. Thus, when we fight about education, we indeed are fighting for our lives. (p. 16)

In my mind, there is no believable explanation for this achievement discrepancy other than that the culture, strengths, talents, and needs of economically disadvantaged African American students are not recognized in schools. In addition (and equally as important), we teachers of African American children may have unintentional biases that interfere with our ability to support these students.

I am not saying that we are all racist. However, when we really stop and think about the history of African American people in this country, we can't help but consider the possibility that somewhere deep down inside of each and every one of us—especially those of us who are White—are some patronizing, distorted attitudes toward and perceptions of African American people. The attitudes manifest themselves in secret reservations we may have about our African American students' potential for high achievement and in the ways we work with them. As I described earlier (see chapter 2), from the time I first started teaching, I had unconscious racist attitudes myself.

Here is one example of the subtle distinction in our perceptions of African American versus White students, a distinction rarely made public but sometimes shared behind closed doors. A White teacher acquaintance of mine was teaching in an inner-city school with a majority of African American students. She learned about an opening for a teaching position at another middle school in an upper-income area with mostly White students. When she met with an administrator in that district, she told him she was really torn between staying and working with the African American students, whom she was enjoying very much, and moving to this new school. The administrator (who was White) told her to understand that if she moved to the school in his district she would be teaching the future leaders of the country, which would certainly not be the case with her African American students. I reacted to this story with dismay and, upon reflection, considered the real possibility that such an attitude might be commonplace.

In light of the existence of such attitudes and perceptions, and based on my own experiences with my African American students and with Jennifer as a collaborator, I have become convinced that some kind of process such as the one we went through, working through racial and cultural differences, is essential in order to change the disproportionate failure rate of African American students in this country. It is essential for us to overcome any barriers—including stereotypes and misconceptions—that may exist between our students and us so that we can offer them the high quality of education and the opportunities for success that all students deserve.

I think you will agree that Hanssen (1998) captures the essence of this vision when she writes about her own process of change:

> I am trying to listen to people of color, both public leaders and my own students. As much as possible, I am working to break through the walls of discomfort and mistrust to engage in honest conversations. And I am constantly on the lookout for the possibility of developing professional relationships with educators of color. I suspect that it will be in collaboration with one of these colleagues that I may discover the most significant contributions I can make. (p. 697)

JENNIFER'S LETTER

I am not a "special" African American teacher. In fact, I am a teacher with few years of experience in school settings. However, I felt that I had advice and guidance to give Karen when she asked me into her classroom. Mostly I cared deeply enough about the intellectual well-being of African American children that I became willing to do whatever was necessary to help another person be the best teacher for these students—-particularly when she also demonstrated the willingness to do whatever was necessary.

I entered the teaching profession thinking I didn't need to work with unsuccessful teachers of African American students—particularly White teachers—but instead could "fix" whatever damage had been done during the time that these children were in their classrooms once they entered mine. This is an arrogant way to think. Every second that a child is in a less than supportive school environment, he or she is adversely affected in ways that are immeasurable. A similar principle applies in reverse:

every second that a child is taught well, loved, and feels cared for, he or she benefits immeasurably. Thus, it becomes imperative for all of us who say that we care to make whatever sacrifices are necessary to ensure that our children experience far more occasions of learning, love, and care than they do of miseducation, frustration, and hurt in their schooling.

I am quick to add, however, that mentors cannot help teachers of African American children who *do not want to be taught,* and I do not believe that any time should be spent convincing such teachers that these kinds of collaborations are what they need. Rather, such processes should evolve from a teacher who observes a potential mentor (perhaps a fellow teacher or a community worker with this student population), becomes convinced about the value of learning from the mentor, and seeks his or her help. That way, the teacher's desire to learn is evident; and upon the mentor's agreeing to such a collaboration, it is clear that both parties are mutually invested from the start. Mutual investment becomes crucial in the particularly tough moments that are inevitable in such a collaborative process.

Finally, I've learned how necessary such collaborations are—among people of all races and cultures and especially in education—to change the legacy of bad racial relations in the United States. We can do it. Karen's and my collaboration was not easy but it was well worth the challenges, to improve pedagogy and teaching practices, and thereby enhance the educational achievement of African American children.

TEACHER COLLABORATION IN THE CLASSROOM

As everyone who has tried it knows, collaboration in the classroom is not easy. Jennifer's and Karen's experience was no exception. As we reflected back on the difficulties we had—especially in the beginning of our collaboration—we realized that there were some specific guiding principles at work that contributed to our perseverance and ultimate success. In light of this, we have identified four guiding principles that we believe are conducive to a successful collaboration between a teacher of African American students and a mentor.

GUIDING PRINCIPLES

1. Mentor teachers should be familiar with the backgrounds of the students being observed. Without that familiarity with their culture and history, an observer is not in a position to give salient advice to the practicing teacher. The practicing teacher may be contributing to the

classroom problems through a lack of awareness of racial and cultural differences, and an observer who has such an awareness can provide the teacher with insight.

2. The teacher should observe the mentor as a classroom teacher in order to know whether he or she is effective with the same student population. If the practicing teacher does not respect the classroom environment and teaching style of the mentor, then questions and suggestions will not be taken seriously, and the teacher will not be receptive to the mentor's impressions of the teacher-student dynamic.

3. The practicing teacher should pick a mentor who has a reputation among colleagues as a successful and effective teacher of these students. That reputation will give stronger credibility to the mentor's comments and insights.

4. The mentor should have some knowledge of action research methods. This recommendation is not as critical as the first three guiding principles, but it is helpful to the process. In our case, Karen was the teacher with that experience, and she and Jennifer designed their methodology as they went along, based on Karen's previous experience.

PREDICTABLE POINTS OF CONFLICT

When we met with Lisa Delpit to discuss our work together and this book, she suggested that in a collaboration such as ours there were bound to be "predictable points of conflict." As we considered such a notion, we identified five examples of such critical crossroads in our collaboration:

1. *Communication styles.* As we described in chapter 3, we each had a very different philosophy about how to handle any discomfort we were experiencing related to the work we were doing. Karen thought it would be better to share the conflicts with friends in order to sort out her feelings and to try to problem-solve the situation with them. Jennifer, however, was expecting that if either one of us was feeling upset or in any way uncomfortable with any aspect of the study, we would reveal our feelings to each other and work at resolving our differences. Such incompatible communication styles could sabotage a collaboration—and nearly did.

2. *Giving and taking of criticism.* One of Karen's biggest challenges (see chapter 3) was hearing and accepting the negative impressions of Karen's teaching that Jennifer shared with her—especially in the beginning of the year. Karen thought of herself as a veteran teacher with a strong reputation in her district and had many memories of praise and accolades for her teaching style. With her African American students, Karen

knew she was not having the kind of satisfactory results she had experienced with her White students, but she did not anticipate or welcome the extent of criticism and questioning that she received from Jennifer. We recommend that when two individuals enter into a classroom collaboration such as ours, they talk about their expectations for the observation comments (oral and written), and that the notes include a respectful awareness of the teacher's expertise and knowledge along with questions and suggestions for improvement. Also, any criticism— which is always difficult to receive—should be carefully and thoroughly explained so that the practicing teacher has a clear sense of what assumptions and expectations are supporting the criticisms. Checking with the students (through surveys, open discussions, interviews, etc.) regarding questions and criticism helps to either validate or discredit the mentor's observations. We urge any potential collaborators to discuss their expectations in these areas before embarking on their collaboration.

3. *Observations by a colleague.* Teaching under any circumstances is challenging, and classroom experiences don't always go smoothly. Karen found that teaching African American students was sometimes a struggle. Having Jennifer in the classroom once a week was not always comfortable. Sometimes Karen became frustrated, and occasionally, she said things or made decisions that she later regretted. It was hard enough to be aware of those problems on her own, but having Jennifer witness what Karen considered to be incompetent teaching made her feel even more vulnerable and inept. We think it is extremely important that the observed teacher reveal such difficult feelings to the mentor so that the mentor is aware of the impact his or her presence is having on the teacher's sense of self. As Karen illustrates, it was not easy to acknowledge such feelings to Jennifer, but she realized it was important in order to build trust in the relationship.

4. *Preconceived notions.* Because of our racial and cultural differences, we each had expectations about how open the other would be in our relationship as collaborators. In the beginning of our study, Karen became suspicious of Jennifer's intentions and motives when Jennifer presented her with an ongoing critique of her teaching. Karen, having had few relationships with African American adults, wondered whether she could trust Jennifer to be fair and objective. Karen worried that Jennifer identified so closely with the students—given their shared racial and cultural background—that she was becoming their advocate, giving little consideration or respect to Karen's point of view. Similarly, Jennifer had assumptions about Karen's ability to effectively teach her African American students and to establish a positive rapport with

them. She questioned whether Karen would be able to recognize hidden racism and prejudice within her own assumptions about her students. These preconceived notions that Jennifer brought with her to our study came from interactions she had had with other White people during her life.

5. *The emergence of fear in the relationship.* In chapter 5, we both talked about fears we experienced as part of the risks we took in working together. We described the fear that our attempts to bridge the gap between White teachers and African American students might not succeed—at least in Karen's case. Karen described a fear of the vulnerability she would feel as the key subject of classroom research, a very threatening prospect to her. Jennifer described a fear of possible repercussions in her academic career as a result of working with a White colleague. We want to emphasize that these or similar fears will surface during any such partnership. Two educators, collaborating in this fashion, whether or not theirs is a cross-racial–cross-cultural partnership, will inevitably have some strong concerns. Based on our own experience, we strongly recommend that these fears be dealt with on a regular basis from the outset, as they arise. Burying them only allows them to grow stronger.

BUILDING TRUST

In this section we'll elaborate on the notion of building trust, since we see it as vital to the collaborative process. The initial trust that began our relationship was based on mutual respect for our professional backgrounds. We were graduate students in the same doctoral program, and this gave us a point of connection as we got to know each other.

At the beginning of our work together, real trust had not been established between us. However, as we got past each pivotal moment and stayed with the process despite our discomfort, the trust grew. Karen began to trust that Jennifer was not deliberately trying to sabotage her. Jennifer began to trust that Karen really wanted to make her classroom a more conducive learning environment for her African American students. And these points of trust were tested again and again, even as the bond between us grew stronger.

What we've learned from this process is that building trust starts with a willingness on the part of both parties to be "vulnerable enough to allow our world to turn upside down in order to allow the realities of others to edge themselves into our consciousness" (Delpit, 1995, p. 342). Trust continues when one protects the vulnerability of the other while still holding high expectations for the other to grow. Finally, trust continues to be nurtured when growth and development in the area that the collaboration was formed to address (in our case, teaching African American students) is evident. The growth and development of the practicing teacher (demonstrated by changes in his or her pedagogy, teaching practices, and interactions with students) build the trust. Moreover, once the partners have met the unpleasant challenge of openly airing their fears or grievances, and the partnership has survived, the trust is there that they'll survive the next challenge. We offer five specific strategies for helping to build trust during the collaborative process:

1. *Engage in constant and honest dialogue.* Talking to each other under all circumstances is critical. Don't assume that both of you are on the same page at any time. Rather, ask the most mundane questions to avoid any misunderstandings. This is particularly important in the early stages of the collaboration when the trust between the two teachers is likely to be quite fragile. Honest dialogue includes conveying to the practicing teacher as much information as possible about the weak areas of his or her teaching. In order for this process to work, the critical feedback (supported with detailed observation notes) cannot be sugarcoated. Honest dialogue holds the potential for one person to offend the other and relies on the offended person's ability to react. If in the process communication breaks down, honest dialogue means talking about *how* to dialogue. Moreover, if dialogue is really honest, one or both of the parties will also know when the dialogue needs help from another source, and here is where the feedback from the students is helpful.

2. *Get feedback from students.* Soliciting students' opinions is sometimes helpful at a point of conflict between the two teachers, especially regarding disagreements about what is occurring in the classroom. This feedback is mentioned here because if the conflict is thus resolved, the process can continue. In the event that students' feedback is insufficient to resolve a conflict, or seems inappropriate, seeking the help of an outside person can be another strategy.

3. *Get feedback from a third party.* In the event that an outsider's opinion is sought, this third person should be knowledgeable about the collaboration and the goals that it was developed to accomplish; have the best interest of both teachers at heart; and be a choice agreed upon by both teachers. Even if both parties know and trust the person, taking the conflict out of the classroom should be a jointly made decision. This is something we did not do, but one that we both agree, in hindsight, is the best strategy for getting outside advice. This joint decision making is a pivotal point of trust building as well as a demonstration of care for each other's vulnerable positions.

4. *Maintain a sense of humor.* Another important strategy is maintaining a sense of humor—in particular, the ability to laugh at yourself. If both people become stubborn and inflexible about their point of view, there won't be room for trust to grow. A sense of humor makes space for one or both teachers to admit that they might be wrong.

5. *Break bread together.* Having a meal together is another strategy for moving the process along. We recommend that the two teachers try to do this at least once a month. Having lunch after particularly rough mornings in the classroom was very helpful to us during our process. Getting out of the classroom affords some distance from the process, and at times this distance is necessary. Conversation across a table of food allows the conversation to expand to other areas of your lives and thereby allows the two of you to know each other better. We found that breaking bread together was an occasion for reaffirming our commitment to the collaboration and reminding ourselves of our ultimate goal.

MAKING CHANGES IN TEACHER EDUCATION PROGRAMS

Beginning in the 1970s, universities and colleges seeking accreditation of their professional programs had to demonstrate that their curricula addressed multiculturalism by educating prospective teachers to work with students from ethnically and culturally diverse backgrounds (Goodwin, 1997). Despite the existence of this requirement, the concept of multicultural teacher education has made little progress. In an investigation of 59 institutions, Gollnick (1992) found that only 56% of the professional education curriculums sufficiently addressed cultural diversity by adequately preparing teachers to work comfortably with diverse students.

Today, more than ever, there is a great need for teachers who can effectively serve diverse student populations. The role of teacher education programs in preparing such teachers is vital, and this lends an urgency to changing these programs. We feel that the lessons learned from this study have implications for the preparation of teachers to work with students who are from racial and cultural backgrounds different from their own.

DIVERSITY AS PART OF THE CURRICULUM

Studies have shown that the majority of prospective teachers who enter certification programs have little knowledge about diverse groups in the United States (Cochran-Smith, 1991; Evertson, 1990; Goodwin, 1997; Melnick & Zeichner, 1997). Overall, teacher candidates and beginning teachers know little about the histories and cultures of culturally diverse groups, and about the discrimination and disenfranchisement that they have encountered. Thus, in preparing teacher candidates to effectively serve diverse student populations in urban public schools, teacher education programs must attend to student teachers' lack of prior knowledge in their curriculum. Goodwin (1997) writes that for teacher candidates to develop as multicultural people and teachers, they must become familiar with racial and ethnic group experiences other than their own. This knowledge base will in turn help teachers address their students' various educational needs and initiate social change through an effective pedagogy.

TEACHER REFLECTION

Moreover, regarding the development of a successful pedagogy, another important component must be included in teacher education programs. This component is teachers' reflection about their own cultural biases and assumptions. In order for preservice teachers to constructively and effectively assist students from diverse ethnic, racial, and cultural backgrounds, they must be given opportunities during the course of their teacher education programs to thoroughly comprehend and explore their own cultural and personal values, their identities, and their social beliefs (Weiner, 1993). The rationale for such an emphasis in teacher education programs is demonstrated by the processes and experiences detailed in this book. We believe that the classroom in a teacher education program would be a great place to cultivate collaborations such as the one we described. Including such collaborations would also enhance the field experiences that are already a part of many teacher education programs.

FIELD AND COMMUNITY EXPERIENCES

Field experiences are among the many ways that teacher education programs can and should prepare teacher candidates to work in racially and culturally diverse settings. In her analysis of teacher preparation programs and clinical experiences, Evertson (1990) found that the field experience requirement of professional education has significantly increased in the past 30 years. Because field experiences constitute such a large component of teacher education, it is necessary that they are meaningful and educative.

Many teacher education programs in the United States include relatively brief or poorly structured community experiences. If teacher candidates spend too little time in culturally diverse environments, community experiences can actually reinforce stereotypes and misconceptions (Melnick & Zeichner, 1997). We feel that the model of the mentoring relationship that resulted from our study would greatly enhance community experiences for teacher candidates. Not only could the mentor assist the field experience in the classroom (along with the master teacher, if the mentor turns out to be someone other than the master teacher), but mentoring could be extended beyond the classroom, with the mentor helping teacher candidates become acquainted with students' lives and communities outside of school. Integrating such experiences in teacher preparation programs places new teachers many steps ahead in being able to address their students' needs in the classroom.

Finally, despite the widely recognized need for more skilled and effective teachers of diverse student populations in urban settings, professional education programs still do not sufficiently address this need. We suggest that teacher candidates need to be prepared multiculturally, in the development of a multicultural knowledge base. Additionally, we believe that incorporating community members as mentors of teacher candidates within teacher education programs would have a significant and positive impact on teacher candidates' knowledge about their future students. This way of knowing students has the potential to improve teacher-student relationships and, ultimately, students' academic achievement.

A FINAL SUMMARY

This book has been the story of how two teachers, in examining the racial and cultural differences between a White teacher and her African American students, found and struggled with those same differences between them as individuals. The differences between Karen and her students influenced the way she was teaching them, the way they responded, and how these interactions potentially affected her students' academic achievement. The same differences between us made our collaboration difficult and threatened to bring it to a halt.

When we came together to do this work, we were in very different places in our teaching careers and in our previous experiences with African American students. We both brought important experiential knowledge to our collaboration, and we both were enriched by the partnership that we developed over the years.

Our story is a difficult and complex one to tell because it has been quite an emotional process for both of us. Singly and simultaneously, we have each experienced such difficult emotions as frustration, confusion, pain, suspicion, disillusionment, fear, anxiety, and anger. On the other hand, we have each found the process to be encouraging, rewarding, moving, thought provoking, and invaluable.

We want to stress how similar our two experiences have been during this process; the toll it took as we recognized and then grappled with our differences was immense for each of us. We also want to stress the enormously important benefits we have gained from this experience. Karen is not proud of the kind of teacher she was with her African American students in the beginning, but what both of us are proud of is what she and Jennifer did about it. Karen recognized a problem; she wasn't as effective with her African American students as she had been with her White students. Her previously successful career as a teacher of White students helped her to recognize the differences, but she decided that she needed help to change the situation with her African American students. Through her collaboration with Jennifer, Karen discovered that her lack of familiarity and comfort with the racial and cultural differences that existed between her and her students were largely responsible for her inability to teach them effectively. From the design of lessons and her style of daily interactions in particular, Karen came to realize that she was contributing to her students' resistance to her. However, through her own determination and Jennifer's perseverance, she was able to overcome the barriers and to grow and change and become a better teacher for her students.

This, then, is ultimately a story of success against many odds—of two women, one African American and one White, battling preconceived notions, prejudices, and unfair expectations about each other. We eventually began to understand and trust each other and gradually became the close friends that we are today. Most important, we learned about the work that is vital and necessary for teachers to do in order to effectively educate all of their students, even those who are the most racially and culturally different from themselves (see also the work of Goodwin [1997], Nieto [1992], and Weiner [1993]).

We believe that the process that we initiated and continued for 3 years is a critical experience for both beginning and veteran teachers across color and class lines. It is a process that should be incorporated into teacher education programs that train teachers for urban schools and into staff development in urban schools. It is a process that holds the potential to help White teachers—as well as all middle-class teachers—to overcome the kind of "cross-cultural disorientation" that Karen describes: the confusion and lack of understanding that she experienced when first working with African American students as a result of their communication style, language use, and behaviors, which she was not accustomed to. Sharing cultural perspectives provides teachers with a different view of their students' behavior, as well as their own. That broadened perspective fosters and maintains a meaningful teacher-student relationship, leading to higher student motivation and achievement and greater teacher satisfaction.

It is our deeply felt hope that those of you reading this book who find yourselves resonating with our beliefs will seriously consider the kind of journey that we experienced together. We believe that our story will help your process if you choose to become a part of such a collaboration. Your challenges may be different from ours, but we hope that reading about ours will give you some support and encouragement in your most crucial moments. For us, it is a question of our willingness to wrestle with these extremely sensitive issues raised in this book, to experience some painful moments along the way, and, *because of the kids,* to persevere until we are confident that we have become the best teachers possible. Every one of us has the power to make a difference in the lives of our students.

Appendix

THEORETICAL FRAMEWORK

In thinking about the nature of our classroom work together, we identified three theoretical perspectives that framed our research. The first theoretical perspective is that the beliefs, intentions, and personalities of all teachers play a more significant role in the success or failure of individual students than the curriculum, materials, class size, and so forth (Fine, 1991; Giroux, 1988; Irvine, 1990). This theory suggests that as individual teachers change their own teaching attitudes and strategies, the entire system of education inevitably shifts to some degree, and the students' success rate can be affected. However, with the disproportionate number of middle-class White teachers working with low-income African American students, racial and cultural differences can make effective change an especially difficult task.

The second theoretical perspective is that unintentional biases of White teachers may undermine the potentially positive processes of teaching and learning described above (Boateng, 1990; Cummins, 1986; Tatum, 1992). As Paley (1979) notes in *White Teacher*, the challenge is "to find a way of communicating to each child the idea that his or her special quality is understood, is valued, and can be talked about" (p. xvi). However, Paley also points out the difficulty of this challenge in a society that is "influenced by the fears and prejudices, apprehensions and expectations, which have become a carefully hidden part of every one of us" (p. xvi).

The third perspective is that since White teachers, like Karen, have such enormous influence over the education of African American children, they should be involved in making the changes that will address the achievement gap. However, the challenges to White teachers of such reform efforts are considerable given that many of them are often not prepared professionally to effectively work with students of color (Delpit, 1995; Fuller, 1994; Obidah & Teel, 1996; Reed, 1996; Valli, 1995). This lack of preparation can be detrimental to the successful academic achievement of these students. Hence, good intentions alone on the part of teachers may not be enough, given the racist nature of American society. Because of their powerful potential to influence students' lives, teachers need to make conscious efforts to recognize the subtle and unintentional biases in their own behavior. Uncovering Karen's subtle and unintentional biases and addressing the racial and cultural differences between Karen and her students were the initial goals of our study. We also came to realize, however, that part of this study included addressing racial and cultural differences between us.

DOING THE RESEARCH

The primary research method of this study was a qualitative approach called teacher research. In recent years, teacher research has become a recognized mode of inquiry with a potential for yielding rich insights and a legitimate knowledge base for the study of teaching, learning, and the process of education in general (Bullough & Gitlin, 1995; Cochran-Smith & Lytle, 1993; Connelly & Clandinin, 1990; Hollingsworth et al., 1994). Teachers' experiences, carefully documented, can reveal the complexities inherent in teaching and suggest conceptual frameworks derived from hours of observations, conversations with students, reflection, and sharing with other teachers.

As teachers, we implement the lesson plans we have designed, and if they are not effective, we have the responsibility for improving them; as researchers, we try to assess, analyze, and explain theoretically the students' responses to the lessons. Based on her experiences with this dual role, Lampert (1991) describes some possible dilemmas:

> So far, I have been talking about how being a teacher affects how I teach. Writing in a voice that allows me to move back and forth between two sets of values and two sets of norms for how one talks about phenomena involves me as a teacher in seeing the events that occur in my classroom in two ways. I bring the curiosity of the research community together with the responsibility of the teaching community, and sometimes these values clash—not only in what I write, but in my thinking about what to do. (p. 9)

Because of the difficulty of the teacher researcher's dual role, we believe that the outside observer's role should be to verify, make problematic, or question the teacher researcher's impressions of the students' responses to classroom experiences. Thus, the teacher researcher's descriptions and conclusions cannot take on the same credibility when they stand alone, untested. When the teacher researcher's findings are validated by the outside observer, they assume a sufficiently different and stronger stature.

In addition to using our teacher research process as a way of gaining insight into Karen's relationship with her students, we also agreed that any immediate findings would be used for changes and improvements to enhance classroom teaching and learning. Thus, since we implemented changes based on the research findings, we were using a process called "Teacher Action Research" (Bullough & Gitlin, 1995; McNiff, Lomax, & Whitehead, 1996; Mills, 2000).

In the remaining pages, beginning with descriptions of the middle school and Karen's classroom, we discuss our research methods.

THE SCHOOL

Harriet Jacobs Middle School, where this study was conducted, is part of the Foothill school district in the San Francisco Bay Area (all names of districts, schools, and students are pseudonyms). The school is located in an area of the district populated mostly by middle-class White families. Between 1985 and 1989, the African American student population at Jacobs increased from 49 to 68%. In 1992, 62% of the Jacobs student body was African American. Many of the African American students and other students of color who lived in the lower-income, downtown areas of the district and attended Jacobs came to and from school on public transportation. The enrollment at Jacobs averaged around 730 students until it became a middle school during the 1991–1992 school year and added a sixth grade to its existing seventh and eighth grades.

THE CLASSROOM

Karen's classes were held in the portable buildings of the school, located between the main school building and the physical education field, although somewhat closer to the field. The portables are fairly large classrooms with windows on either side. Karen taught for two rather than five periods each day, and classes were 50 minutes long.

When one entered Karen's classroom it was clear that history was the subject being taught. Pictures depicting the rise and fall of the Roman Empire, the three ancient empires of West Africa, and other historical moments in time were brightly displayed on the walls. On the side of the room closest to the door there was an extensive library, mostly fiction and autobiography, all books having a historic theme. A small sign on each shelf of the bookcase indicated the ethnic origins of the books on that shelf. Under a table alongside one wall of the room was a box of games, also with historic themes.

Karen had carefully structured lesson plans. Every day when the students came into the class, the first 5 minutes was theirs, to settle down and get themselves ready for the lesson. When students entered the class they saw an agenda on the board that informed them of the class activities for that day. Examples of Karen's classroom agenda on the first days of the school year are as follows:

Thursday, September 2, 1993
Agenda:
1) Roll
2) Read for 10 minutes (*Ebony, Jet, Newsweek,* or book)
3) Fill out reading cards
4) Make folders
5) Discuss class policy

Friday, September 3, 1993
Agenda:
1) Roll
2) Read for 10 minutes
3) Reading cards
4) Class policy
5) Per. 3: Finish questions from Wed.
   Per. 5: Map assignment

The class would begin with the designated student historian. This student would read notes that he or she had written about the previous day's classroom activities. Overall, the classroom seemed to be a place of inviting warmth.

RESEARCH METHODS

DATA COLLECTION

During the first year of our 3-year study, our data included systematic classroom observations by Jennifer, Karen's written responses to Jennifer's notes and analyses, student questionnaires, informal interviews, biweekly meetings, and the feedback from presentations of our work at various conferences.

We gathered data that first year from two different cohorts of approximately 30 students in each of two seventh-grade world history classes taught by Karen. Eighty percent of the students were African American and the other 20% were made up of about equal proportions of Hispanic, Asian, and White students.

CLASSROOM OBSERVATIONS. During the first semester of the school year, Jennifer attended Karen's classroom once a week on Wednesdays. During the second semester she went to the classroom twice a week, on Tuesdays and Thursdays. Jennifer recorded many examples of students' interactions with Karen as well as their interactions with one another. She recorded these events along with her tentative analysis of what she thought had occurred in those moments.

In the 2nd year Karen taught only one class. Once again, her students were primarily African American. She kept daily journal notes of her own observations, and Jennifer attended and observed in Karen's classroom for 2 weeks at the beginning of each quarter. She substituted for Karen on occasion as well.

In the 3rd year of our study, Karen wrote daily journal entries, and another classroom teacher at her school wrote observation notes and an analysis every day as well. Karen mailed these data to Jennifer, and Jennifer gave her feedback. We corresponded by E-mail as well.

WRITTEN RESPONSES. During the 1st year of our study, Jennifer gave Karen weekly write-ups of her observations. Initially we discussed whether to exchange notes every week or every month. We decided to do so every week, because we both believed that the feedback was invaluable to the practice of teaching, and the more timely the feedback the better. However, this exchange of data revealed some of Karen's expectations for feedback, as shown in the following:

JENNIFER'S OBSERVATIONS

Period 3: She tells students that they are going to do a questionnaire. About 21 students came early. The bell rings and 1 or 2 students run to their seat [to be "on time" to class meant that students had to be in their seats when the bell rang]. More students seem to be absent in class today than there were last week on Wednesday. During the 10 minute reading period, most of the students are really reading. An African American male student is talking with an African American female student across from him. Ten students are really reading, that is, seemingly engaged in a book. The other students are doing various things, ranging from leafing through a book to not opening a book at all, but the whole class is quiet. One student is talking. Overall, the reading time was good.

One African American female student is talking with another African American female student about Karen calling home: "She was supposed to be calling my house to say I'm late. She say I don't do my homework [this student seems to think that Karen oversteps her boundaries when she calls their house, i.e. Karen says she's calling about one thing and then when she calls she mentions other things, not necessarily what she said she was going to call about]. [10/20/93]

KAREN'S RESPONSE

What do you think of the reading program so far in terms of my goal of continually validating cultural differences among the students?

Based on what one of the students said about what I talk about with their parents or guardians over the phone, I guess I need to clarify my intentions when I call home: to talk about the "whole" student, both positive traits and the need for improvement in various areas. [10/20/93]

This was the process by which Karen responded to Jennifer's notes, and Jennifer in turn responded to her notes. In this way also, the data became a dynamic part of the teaching practice. In fact, as shown in the second excerpt from Karen's response, some changes in teacher-student relations came into effect based on observations emerging from the research methodology.

We both attempted to build relationships with the young people outside of their role as students and our role as the teacher researchers. This was done during lunchtime when at least a third of the 5th-period students would come into the classroom. Jennifer also took notes on some of the lunchtime interactions between Karen and her students as shown in the following excerpts:

I came to Jacobs at lunch time. There were 12 students in the class during lunch. Some eating and some sitting at their desks leafing through a book from the classroom library and others talking to each other or talking to Karen. It seems that good bonds are forming between Karen and the students that spill over into the class time. More of the 5th period students come in during lunch time than the 3rd period class. [12/8/93]

Here are some of Karen's own thoughts about the lunchtime activities:

During lunch time I see the students in a completely different light, and I'm sure they see me differently too [we should verify that in the next questionnaire or in interviews]. The topics that are discussed are more of a personal nature, and I learn more about their interests and concerns. This time is an excellent time for me to casually talk to the students about the class, about their perceptions of the grades, about their perceptions of me as their teacher, etc. I have got to take more advantage of that very special time with my students. [1/18/93]

We both used lunchtime as an opportunity to get to know the students better, although tensions arose between us about whether Jennifer should share information from the students with Karen. We also had to address the potential for the development of a dynamic such as the students and Jennifer against Karen.

STUDENT QUESTIONNAIRES. During the 1st year, we administered two questionnaires to the students. The first one was composed of questions about the students' perceptions of race and class differences between them and Karen and among their peers, their perceptions of classroom organization, and Karen's teaching practices. The second questionnaire was a follow-up on some of the aspects of Karen's class that the students had noted as problematic in the first questionnaire.

We decided that Jennifer would administer the questionnaires to the students with Karen out of the classroom. We decided on this for two reasons: First, we did not want the students to feel self-conscious about talking about and writing down their honest feelings about their teacher, Karen. Second, since the questionnaires were to be answered anonymously, we wanted to reassure the students as much as possible that their answers would not affect their grade or Karen's attitude toward them.

INFORMAL INTERVIEWS. Informal interviews took place throughout the 1st year of the study and were utilized to address a specific issue that came up between Karen and her students. For example, when disruptions occurred in the class and the cause was not clear, Jennifer would informally interview members of the class to find out what students were reacting to (data from such an interview is included in chapter 4).

BIWEEKLY MEETINGS. We met on a biweekly basis over the course of the first year to discuss the classroom experiences. As a component of some of these meetings, we had lunch together to talk about events that occurred in the classroom. Our lunchtime conversations were varied, and sometimes we taped and transcribed them. We talked about the students' behavior toward Karen. We looked at student behavior as a result of recent events that took place in the classroom. Sometimes we discussed students' possible perceptions based on previous classroom experiences that they brought with them to her classroom. We found an example of this to be the ideas that African American teachers are more strict than White teachers and that White teachers are oftentimes afraid of African American students.

On other days Karen followed up on something that Jennifer may have said to the students, or Jennifer voiced some of her observations. During these and other times we talked about our own personal racial, class, and cultural biases, trying to identify the "baggage" we might be bringing to the research. As a result, many aspects of our research methodology were negotiated in this way, and conflict regularly occurred. We described these dynamics in more detail when we discussed the "critical moments in teacher research" in chapter 3.

FEEDBACK FROM PRESENTATIONS. As the years went by, we spoke at a number of conferences and smaller gatherings, addressing groups composed of university professors, teacher educators, classroom teachers, student teachers, and graduate students. In 1995, we gave presentations at AERA in San Francisco, at the International Teacher as Researcher Conference held at the University of California, Davis, and at a conference on educational change at the University of South Africa in Pretoria. In 1996, we spoke at AERA in New York, and in 1997, we gave an invited talk to educators at Holy Names College in Oakland, California. We also shared our research experience with teachers at the university lab school at the University of California, Los Angeles, and with student teachers at UC Berkeley and at Saint Mary's College in northern California.

Over the years some of these presentations were videotaped. We also asked the audience for written feedback. We considered these as additional data for our study. These experiences helped each of us to crystallize our thinking about the purpose of our work together and its impact on the students, on each of us as individual teacher researchers, and on our collaborative relationship as a teacher research team.

DATA ANALYSIS

In terms of data analysis, in the first year of our study, Jennifer's class-room observations, Karen's responses, the informal interview data, and the data from the questionnaires were coded and summarized monthly using a constant comparative approach (Glaser & Strauss, 1967). According to the constant comparative approach, as data are collected over a designated period of time, the researcher determines tentative results. Then, as new data are collected, the researcher constantly compares those results with the earlier tentative findings and adjusts the "current findings" accordingly. For example, every week the two separate sets of notes were compared by each of us for similarities and differences in findings.

There were three coding categories used for data analysis: (1) student and teacher racial and cultural expectations, (2) teacher and student motivation, and (3) students and teacher rapport. As time passed, overall changes were also recorded. In addition, the students' questionnaires and interviews along with other teacher data were coded and summarized for salient themes by an independent data analyst as they were collected. At the end of the school year, those themes that reoccurred regularly across all data sources became the basis for final conclusions and recommendations.

References

Alleyne Johnson [Obidah], J. (1995a). *Teachable moments, constructed identities, and classroom conflict: Toward a critical teaching practice.* Unpublished dissertation, University of California, Berkeley.

Alleyne Johnson [Obidah], J. (1995b). Life after death: Critical pedagogy in an urban classroom. *Harvard Educational Review, 65,* 213–230.

Baldwin, J. (1996). A talk to teachers. Reprinted in W. Ayers & P. Ford (Eds.), *City kids, city teachers: Reports from the front row* (pp. 219–227). New York: New Press.

Boateng, F. (1990). Combating deculturalization of the African-American child in the public school system: A multicultural approach. In K. Lomotey (Ed.), *Going to school: The African American experience* (pp. 73–84). Albany: State University of New York Press.

Bullough, R. V., & Gitlin, A. (1995). *Becoming a student of teaching.* New York: Garland.

Cochran-Smith, M. (1991). Learning to teach against the grain. *Harvard Educational Review, 61,* 279–310.

Cochran-Smith, M. (1995a). Uncertain allies: Understanding the boundaries of race and teaching. *Harvard Educational Review, 65,* 541–570.

Cochran-Smith, M. (1995b). Color blindness and basket making are not the answers: Confronting the dilemmas of race, culture, and language diversity in teacher education. *American Educational Research Journal, 32,* 493–522.

Cochran-Smith, M., & Lytle, S. L. (1993). *Inside/outside: Teacher research and knowledge.* New York: Teachers College Press.

Collins, M., & Tamarkin, C. (1982). *Marva Collins' Way.* Los Angeles: J. P. Tarcher.

Connelly, M. F., & Clandinin, D. J. (1990). Stories of experience and narrative inquiry. *Educational Researcher, 19,* 2–13.

Covington, M. V. (1984). The self-worth theory of achievement motivation: Findings and implications. *The Elementary School Journal, 85,* 5–20.

Cummins, J. (1986). Empowering minority students: A framework for intervention. *Harvard Educational Review, 56,* 18–36.

Delpit, L. (1988). The silenced dialogue: Power and pedagogy in educating other people's children. *Harvard Educational Review, 58,* 280–298.

Delpit, L. (1992a). Acquisition of literate discourse: Bowing before the master? *Theory into Practice, 31,* 296–302.

Delpit, L. (1992b). Education in a multicultural society: Our future's greatest challenge. *Journal of Negro Education, 61,* 237–249.

Delpit, L. (1995). *Other people's children: Cultural conflict in the classroom.* New York: New Press.

Edwards, A. (1998, March). Black and White women: What still divides us? *Essence,* pp. 77–78, 80, 136, 138–140.

Evertson, C. M. (1990). Bridging knowledge and action through clinical experiences. In D. D. Dill (Ed.), *What teachers need to know: The knowledge, skills, and values essential to good teaching* (pp. 94–107). San Francisco: Jossey-Bass.

Fine, M. (1987). Silencing in public schools. *Language Arts, 64,* 157–174.

Fine, M. (1991). *Framing dropouts: Notes on the politics of urban public high schools.* Albany: State University of New York Press.

Fordham, S., & Ogbu, J. U. (1986). Black students' school success: Coping with the "burden of 'acting White.'" *The Urban Review, 18,* 176–206.

Fuller, M. L. (1994). The monocultural graduate in the multicultural environment: A challenge for teacher educators. *Journal of Teacher Education, 45,* 269–277.

Gates, H. L., Jr. (1984). The blackness of blackness: A critique of the sign and the signifying monkey. In H. L. Gates, Jr. (Ed.), *Black literature and literary theory* (pp. 285–321). New York: Methuen.

Giroux, H. A. (1988). *Schooling and the struggle for public life.* Minneapolis: University of Minnesota Press.

Glaser, B., & Strauss, A. (1967). *The discovery of grounded theory: Strategies for qualitative research.* New York: Aldine de Gruyter.

Goines, D. L. (1993). *The free speech movement: Coming of age in the 1960s.* Berkeley, CA: Ten Speed Press.

Gollnick, D. M. (1992). Multicultural education: Policies and practices in teacher education. In C. A. Grant (Ed.), *Research and multicultural education: From the margins to the mainstream* (pp. 218–239). London: Falmer Press.

Goodwin, A. L. (1997). Historical and contemporary perspectives on multicultural teacher education: Past lessons, new directions. In J. E. King, E. R. Hollins, & W. C. Hayman (Eds.), *Preparing teachers for cultural diversity* (pp. 5–22). New York: Teachers College Press.

Griffin, J. H. (1960). *Black like me.* New Jersey: New American Library.

Hanssen, E. (1998). A White teacher reflects on institutional racism. *Phi Delta Kappan, 79,* 694–698.

Heath, S. B. (1983). *Ways with words: Language, life, and work in communities and classrooms.* New York: Cambridge University Press.

Hilliard, A., III (1992). Behavioral style, culture, and teaching and learning. *The Journal of Negro Education, 61,* 370–377.

Hollingsworth, S., Cody, A., Davis-Smallwood, J., Dybdahl, M., Gallagher, P., Gallego, M., Maestre, T., Minarik, L., Raffel, L., Standerford, N. S., & Teel, K. M. (1994). *Teacher research and urban literacy education.* New York: Teachers College Press.

Hollins, E. R., & Spencer, K. (1990). Restructuring schools for cultural inclusion:

Changing the schooling process for American youngsters. *Journal of Education, 172,* 89–100.

Irvine, J. J. (1990). *Black students and school failure: Policies, practices and prescriptions.* New York: Greenwood Press.

King, J. (1991). Dysconscious racism: Ideology, identity, and the miseducation of teachers. *The Journal of Negro Education, 60,* 133–146.

King, J., & Ladson-Billings, G. (1990). The teacher education challenge in elite university settings: Developing critical perspectives for teaching in a democratic and multicultural society. *European Journal of Intercultural Studies, 1,* 15–30.

Ladson-Billings, G. (1990). Like lightning in a bottle: Attempting to capture the pedagogical excellence of successful teachers of Black students. *International Journal of Qualitative Studies in Education, 3,* 335–344.

Ladson-Billings, G. (1994). *The dreamkeepers: Successful teachers of African American children.* San Francisco, CA: Jossey-Bass.

Ladson-Billings, G. (1995). Toward a theory of culturally relevant pedagogy. *American Education Research Journal, 32,* 465–491.

Ladson-Billings, G. (1996, April). *Fighting for our lives: Preparing teachers to teach African American children.* Paper presented at the annual meeting of the American Educational Research Association, New York.

Lampert, M. (1991, April). *Knowing and telling about teaching: Paradoxes and problems in being a school teacher and a university researcher.* Paper presented at the annual meeting of the American Educational Research Association, Chicago.

MacLeod, J. (1987). *Ain't no makin' it: Aspirations and attainment in a low-income neighborhood.* Boulder, CO: Westview Press.

Marshall, H. H., & Weinstein, R. S. (1984). Classroom factors affecting students' self-evaluations: An interactional model. *Review of Educational Research, 54,* 301–325.

McCarthy, C., & Crichlow, W. (Eds.). (1993). *Race, identity, and representation in education.* New York: Routledge.

McIntosh, P. (1989, July/August). White privilege: Unpacking the invisible knapsack. *Peace and Freedom, 49,* 10–12.

McNiff, J., Lomax, P., & Whitehead, J. (1996). *You and your action research project.* London: Routledge.

Melnick, S. L., & Zeichner, K. M. (1997). Enhancing the capacity of teacher education institutions to address diversity issues. In J. E. King, E. R. Hollins, & W. C. Hayman (Eds.), *Preparing teachers for cultural diversity* (pp. 23–89). New York: Teachers College Press.

Mills, G. E. (2000). *Action research: A guide for the teacher researcher.* Upper Saddle River, NJ: Prentice Hall.

Mitchell, J. (1996). Reflections of a Black social scientist: Some struggles, some doubts, some hopes. *Harvard Educational Review Reprint Series, 28,* 69–88.

Nieto, S. (1992). *Affirming diversity: The sociopolitical context of multicultural education.* New York: Longman.

Oakes, J. (1985). *Keeping track: How schools structure inequality.* New Haven: Yale University Press.

Obidah, J. (in press). Giving voice to those who look like us but who are not us. In R. Jeffries & G. Givens (Eds.), *African American women as qualitative researchers: Performing acts of understanding and survival.* Hampton, VA: Hampton University Press.

Obidah, J., & Teel, K. M. (1996). The impact of race and cultural differences on the teacher/student relationship: A collaborative classroom study by an African American and Caucasian teacher research team. *Kansas Association for Supervision and Curriculum Development Record, 14,* 70–86.

Ogbu, J., & Matute-Bianchi, M. (1986). Understanding sociocultural factors: Knowledge, identity, and school adjustment. In Evaluation, Dissemination and Assessment Center (California State University), *Beyond language: Social and cultural factors in schooling language minority students.* Los Angeles: Author.

Paley, V. G. (1979). *White teacher.* Cambridge, MA: Harvard University Press.

Reed, D. F. (1996, April). *Speaking from experience: Anglo-American teachers in African American schools.* Paper presented at the annual meeting of the American Educational Research Association, New York.

Rubin, L. B. (1976). *Worlds of pain: Life in the working-class family.* New York: Basic Books.

Sleeter, C. (1993). How white teachers construct race. In C. McCarthy & W. Crichlow (Eds.), *Race, identity and representation in education* (pp. 157–169). New York: Routledge.

Steele, C. M. (1992). Race and the schooling of Black Americans. *Atlantic Monthly, 269,* 68–78.

Tatum, B. D. (1992). Talking about race, learning about racism: The application of racial identity development theory in the classroom. *Harvard Educational Review, 62,* 1–24.

Teel, K. M., & DeBruin-Parecki, A. (2001). *Making school count: Promoting urban student motivation and success.* London: Routledge Falmer.

Teel, K. M., DeBruin-Parecki, A., & Covington, M. V. (1998). Teaching strategies that honor and motivate inner-city African American students: A school/university collaboration. *Teaching and Teacher Education, 14,* 479–495.

Valli, L. (1995). The dilemma of race: Learning to be color blind and color conscious. *Journal of Teacher Education, 46,* 120–129.

Weiner, L. (1993). *Preparing teachers for urban schools: Lessons from thirty years of school reform.* New York: Teachers College Press.

Index

121

,

About the Authors

JENNIFER E. OBIDAH is an assistant professor in the Graduate School of Education and Information Studies at UCLA. Jennifer completed her doctorate at the University of California at Berkeley. In 1995, Jennifer received a National Institute of Mental Health (NIMH) Postdoctoral Fellowship. Her areas of research are the social and cultural contexts of urban schooling, focusing on issues of violence, multicultural education, and teacher preparation. Jennifer is currently the principal investigator of a study that examines the schooling experiences of juvenile delinquents.

KAREN MANHEIM TEEL has been a classroom teacher in the San Francisco Bay Area since 1969, mostly teaching world and U.S. history at the junior high/middle school level. In 1993, she received a doctoral degree in education from the University of California at Berkeley, after conducting dissertation research in her own middle school classroom. In 1994, Karen received a 2-year Spencer Postdoctoral Fellowship to continue her classroom research. She is currently adjunct faculty at Holy Names College in Oakland, California. Her interests are urban education, teacher research, and student motivation.